UNFIREABLE

Unfireable

You Can Be Fired From Your Job, But You Can Never Be Fired From Your Purpose

Dr. Velma Trayham

Published by Game Changer Publishing

Paperback ISBN: 979-8-90158-129-2
Hardcover ISBN: 979-8-90158-130-8
Digital ISBN: 979-8-90158-131-5

www.GameChangerPublishing.com

For Mama Lynn
My praying grandmother, who raised me, covered me, and
saw greatness in me long before I could see it in myself.
May you rest in heaven knowing your prayers built this foundation.

For my mother, Elizabeth Trayham
Your courage, resilience, and love remind me every day that
where we started is not where we have to finish.

And for my dear friend and board member, Joe Lubeck
Your belief in me, partnership, and commitment to impact are woven
throughout the pages of this book and the work it represents.

Thank you for shaping my life, my faith, and my purpose.

Advance Praise

"Dr. Velma Trayham doesn't just offer encouragement—she offers a lifeline during times of uncertainty. This book speaks directly to anyone who feels shaken by a changing job market or a shrinking sense of security. She reminds us that while positions can disappear, purpose does not. She also provides readers (and thousands of individuals across the country) with a steady hand for anyone determined to rise, rebuild, and protect what truly matters."

— **Cameron Robb, Senior Economic Development Consultant, Arizona Public Service**

"'You Can Be Fired From Your Job, But You Can Never Be Fired From Your Purpose' is a bold and necessary message for leaders who refuse to let disruption define their destiny. Dr. Velma Trayham powerfully shows how to separate identity from title, rise with clarity after loss, and lead with authority beyond any single role—igniting executives, entrepreneurs, and mission-driven leaders to rebuild, reimagine, and move forward with unshakeable confidence. This book doesn't just speak to transition; it fuels transformation and lasting impact."

— **Erin Floyd, Senior Vice President, Truist Bank**

"Dr. Velma Trayham has an extraordinary gift for turning crisis into calling, and this book is a powerful roadmap for anyone ready to stop chasing titles and start walking in purpose. Her strategies are exactly what leaders, entrepreneurs, and changemakers need in this economic climate."

— **Tye Hayes, Founder of NOVATE Business Solutions**

"This message is long overdue. In a world shaken by layoffs and uncertainty, Dr. Trayham doesn't just inspire you—she equips you with clear, actionable steps to build a life and business anchored in purpose, not position."

— Marjorie Sabido, Executive Assistant, Black Chamber of Arizona

"Dr. Trayham is a prolific leader who will help you reconnect with what you were born to do: work shaped by your passions, the problems you feel called to solve, and a purpose no job title can take away. If you've ever felt that quiet but persistent pull to move in a new direction, this book will give you clarity, alignment, and the courage to act during transition. I believe this book is a must-read for leaders and professionals who are ready to stop waiting and start building lasting impact."

— Dr. Sharon D. Smith, Vice President, Outreach,
and Partnerships, Arizona State University

"Dr. Trayham is a visionary leader. She combines purpose, passion, and faith in teaching the importance of resilience for business leaders, entrepreneurs, and those in the workforce. Her latest book is a must-read for anyone who has faced adversity—or wants to glean understanding from how others have risen from severe setbacks. The key takeaway: as long as we focus on our purpose, we will ultimately succeed in life and in business. You cannot be fired from your purpose."

— Jessica Pacheco, Founder & Managing Partner of Pacheco Ventures

Read This First

Thank you for investing in this book and in your own journey of purpose. I'd love to stand in agreement with you in prayer as you walk this out.

Scan the QR code to:

- Access a free prayer and additional encouragement
- Visit my website for resources and updates
- Inquire about bulk book orders for your team, church, or organization
- Book me for speaking engagements, trainings, and consulting on purpose-driven leadership and economic empowerment.

UNFIREABLE

You Can Be Fired From Your Job, But You
Can Never Be Fired From Your Purpose

DR. VELMA TRAYHAM

Foreword

By Mónica S. Villalobos, Ed.D.

There are seasons in life when everything familiar is stripped away—titles, security, certainty, and even confidence. It is in those moments, when the ground beneath us feels unsteady, that purpose speaks the loudest. Not as a whisper in comfort but as a call to courage.

I believe with my whole heart that purpose is not discovered in ease—it is revealed in adversity.

As a woman of faith, I have come to understand that God does His deepest work in us when life feels uncertain and uncomfortable. When doors close. When systems fail. When what once defined us is suddenly gone. Those moments are not detours; they are divine invitations to listen more closely, trust more deeply, and step forward more boldly.

That is exactly what Dr. Velma Trayham taps into throughout this book. By sharing her story and allowing us to peer into her wounds, she shows us a path to heal and thrive, triggering our purpose.

Unfireable is more than a message—it is a mandate. Dr. Trayham reminds us that while jobs can be lost, titles can be stripped, and platforms can shift, purpose **is permanent**. Purpose is assigned by our creator. It cannot be downsized, outsourced, or eliminated by any system on earth.

Within these pages, you will find truth told without apology, faith expressed with courage, and wisdom forged through lived experience. This is not theory. It is testimony. It is leadership shaped by loss, resilience refined by rejection, and vision clarified through discipline.

At its core, this book calls each of us to one essential charge: *Pursue* **your** *Purpose* **with** *Passion*.

Not casually. Nor fearfully. Not when conditions are perfect. But with conviction. With urgency. With faith that refuses to shrink in the face of challenge.

You may be reading this at a crossroads, perhaps questioning your directions, grieving a loss, or wondering whether the best of your contribution is behind you. Let me assure you—it is not! Purpose doesn't expire. It evolves. And often, it emerges most clearly when life disrupts our plans so God can reveal His.

This book speaks to the overlooked, the underestimated, the laid-off, the locked-out, and the called-but-hesitant. It is for leaders who sense there must be more. It is for builders, problem-solvers, and visionaries who know that faith without action is incomplete—and action without purpose is empty.

As you turn these pages, I invite you to read, not just with your eyes, but with your spirit. Allow this book to challenge what you have settled on, awaken what you may have buried, and confirm what God has already placed within you.

Because when you understand that your purpose is bigger than your position, stronger than your circumstances, and anchored in something eternal, you become truly unfireable.

May this book stir your faith, strengthen your resolve, and remind you, especially in difficult seasons, that **your purpose is not behind you. It is calling you forward.**

And when it does, pursue it… With courage, with discipline, with passion.

— Mónica S. Villalobos, Ed.D.
President & CEO, Arizona Hispanic Chamber of Commerce

Advance Praise

By Shamia Lodge

Purpose is the one thing systems cannot repossess.

Titles can be stripped. Contracts can be canceled. Roles can be eliminated. Entire industries can be disrupted overnight. But purpose, when it is real, rooted, and lived, cannot be fired.

That truth sits at the heart of *Unfireable.*

We are living in a moment where millions of people are being forced to confront a hard question they were never encouraged to ask while things were "working": Who am I when the system no longer needs me?

For too long, we have allowed institutions to define our worth. We have equated proximity to power with purpose and confused stability with calling. This book disrupts that lie. It does not offer comfort. It offers clarity.

Dr. Velma Trayham writes for the leaders who have been laid off, locked out, passed over, silenced, or underestimated. She writes for the builders who kept showing up even when the applause stopped. She writes for the intrapreneurs, the system shapers, the culture carriers, and the people who have always known they were meant to do more than survive inside broken structures.

What makes Unfireable different is that it does not separate faith from strategy or purpose from execution. It recognizes what many leadership books avoid naming: that calling is not abstract. Calling shows up in boardrooms, budgets, procurement decisions, hiring pipelines, community investment, and the courage to tell the truth when silence would be safer.

This book meets us in the tension between obedience and opportunity.

As someone who has spent my career working at the intersection of systems, leadership, and economic access, I see *Unfireable* as both a personal reckoning and a professional mandate. It reminds us that purpose is not something we discover after loss. It is what carries us through it. It is what allows us to lead change from the inside of companies, communities, and institutions, even when the cost is real.

This is not a book you read casually. It is a book you wrestle with. It asks you to stop outsourcing your identity to organizations and to start honoring the assignment that has been with you long before the title and will remain long after it.

If you are reading the book while uncertain about your future, know this: uncertainty does not cancel purpose. If you are reading this while holding influence, know this too: stewardship requires courage.

You may lose a job. You may lose access. You may lose a platform.

But if you are walking in purpose, you are not finished.

You are unfireable, and this book reminds you why.

— Shamia Lodge
Purpose-Driven Leader

Table of Contents

THE CURRENT CLIMATE: LET'S TELL THE TRUTH

We are living in unprecedented times.

In 2025, the world seems to be turned upside down and filled with chaos. Mass layoffs. Government shutdowns. Boycotts. Sex scandals. Racial tensions are escalating. Mental health issues are at an all-time high, and AI is replacing jobs faster than we can keep up.

Over the last three years, more than 35 million Americans have experienced job displacement. In some sectors, AI and automation have completely eliminated entire departments overnight. Employees with over twenty years of service have been replaced by technology or let go without any explanation.

Economic instability is no longer a crisis; it has become a climate. Diversity and Inclusion programs are being dismantled at an alarming rate. Diversity officers are being terminated, strategic inclusion initiatives are being canceled, and companies are retreating under political pressure. The same executives who once celebrated representation are now scrambling.

The result of this is clear: we have relied on the government and external solutions for far too long. People are desperately trying to plan for their future without a roadmap. Fear is escalating, identities are shaken, and talking about faith is a touchy subject.

Your purpose is the problem that God put you on earth to solve. If you are willing to walk by faith, this may just be your most powerful season yet. You can be fired from your job, but you can never be fired from your purpose.

Pause for a moment and let that thought sink in. Let it disrupt your doubts. Let it provoke your potential.

Let it stir your spirit because the moment of opportunity is right here, right now. This isn't just the start of another book; it marks the beginning of a breakthrough for you and the start of your transformation.

It's the start of a purpose-driven assignment. It's an urgent call to the problem solvers, innovators, disruptors, and leaders who feel they have more to contribute to the world.

This message is for the overlooked, the underestimated, the underdogs, and those who have been laid off or locked out. It is for the dreamers who believe success is not for them. I want you to hear me clearly:

You are not here by accident. You were created and chosen for such a time as this.

This book is for women and men who know they are called but are afraid to take the leap. It's for people who have lost a six-figure job or a seven-figure title and don't know who they are without the corner office.

This book is for the millennials who are tired of waiting for access and are striving to walk in purpose and destiny. This book is for the Gen Z visionaries who have been told they are too young. It is for the baby boomers, who are witnessing the system shift and do not know how to pivot.

This book speaks to corporate leaders who are hiding their gifts behind companies that do not value them. It is for entrepreneurs with multiple ideas but no funding or practical next steps to address the problems they are destined to solve.

This book is for anyone who has just been fired or laid off. It's for the fearless and the frustrated, those who believe in God but are ready for strategic guidance.

If any of this describes you, then welcome.

You have found the sign you have been waiting for.

Now, let me explain why I wrote this book and why you should pay attention. I was born into poverty to a fourteen-year-old mother in Houston, Texas. I experienced poverty, rejection, depression, persecution, pain, dysfunction, and fear. I'm a product of the public school system and a family line of drug addiction, school dropouts, and the list goes on. To add the icing on the cake, my father wasn't in my life, so I had to overcome the orphan spirit. I can talk about it because it's a lived experience.

In the ZIP code where I was born, 77004, nearly 60 percent of residents live below the poverty line, yet I left that environment and built a different future.

I started my entrepreneurial journey out of necessity. Yes, I experienced business failures, not just once but multiple times. I really had to figure life out.

To fast forward, I've become a world-renowned entrepreneur, speaker, and economic empowerment expert. I've stood on stages around the country. I've consulted and advised governments and corporations, and I've created programs to help small businesses rise above the poverty line. I've built and sold companies and helped thousands of others do the same. I've also had the privilege of praying for thousands of people, helping them walk in their true purpose and destiny.

There is so much power in prayer. For three years straight, every Friday morning, whether I was in a hotel room, an airport, or even in a foreign country, I led battle-ready prayer calls with hundreds of participants from around the world. I still do! I feel like it's part of my assignment. I am like Nehemiah on the wall for my Heavenly Father. If you don't know the story of Nehemiah in the Bible, you should definitely read it, although I'll talk about it later in this book.

I serve as the founder of multiple high-performing companies and the visionary behind the nonprofit organization Millionaire Mastermind Academy, where we've trained over eight thousand entrepreneurs in business, leadership, and mindset. I don't share this to impress you; I share it to show you what's possible. If God did it for me, He can do it for you.

You may have been fired from a job in the past, but by the time you finish reading this book, you will understand that you can never be fired from your purpose.

You may have faced rejection or persecution, but once you start walking in your calling, you can never be removed from it.

This book is not just my personal story; it is a blueprint for transformation. Here, you will learn how to break generational curses that manifest as fear, poverty, climbing the corporate ladder with no purpose, false burdens, and procrastination. You will discern the difference between what's right and almost right, because almost right is *wrong*!

You will learn how to build businesses and systems that outlive you, navigate betrayal, slander, and spiritual warfare in leadership, and activate your divine assignment, even if others have counted you out. You'll discover how to sow in faith, reap in purpose, and build a legacy. You will learn how to walk in excellence, not just mere survival.

I will guide you toward becoming a firebrand leader, a leader who refuses to conform to broken systems. I will show you how to create a purpose protection plan that covers your calling, purpose, and destiny. You'll redefine wealth and influence through kingdom strategy. Along the way, you'll encounter data, hear stories, laugh, possibly cry, reflect, and get activated. Most importantly, you'll leave with a roadmap for living the rest of your life.

Now, hear me clearly: Sometimes, we don't realize we've been distracted until it's too late. The enemy's job is to kill your destiny, steal your purpose, and destroy the path God has planned for you. The enemy isn't always obvious; he often acts in subtle ways. He distracts you first, keeping you busy with things that seem beneficial but aren't purposeful.

You may find yourself doing things that don't align with your calling or purpose. Suddenly, you may wake up ten years later, feeling tired and off track, wondering, *Where did all my time go?* There are twenty-four hours in a day. Eight hours should be for sleep and eight for work. What about the other eight hours?

I like to apply this concept to years as well: twenty-four years, with eight years spent sleeping and eight working. What have you done with your time? What impact have you had on the world?

This book serves as a divine disruption, an interruption to help you step into the destiny and the purpose meant for you. It's time to stop merely surviving and start thriving.

I now help public and private organizations build and scale purpose-driven companies and programs. To bring this message to your company, university, or city, you can book me for keynotes, trainings, and consulting using the information at the back of this book.

It's time to begin solving problems; the world is waiting for your purpose.

Let me conclude this introduction by saying this: I understand fear, betrayal, and the pain of crying in silence while trying to walk by faith. I know the cost of carrying a calling that others may not comprehend.

I understand this: walking in purpose brings rewards, not just financially but also in terms of legacy. I want to help you discover your purpose. Let's work together and rise emotionally and positionally.

The systems in this world are flawed, but you were meant to create new ones. While you can lose your job, you can never be fired from your purpose once you truly embrace it. The world is waiting for the unique solution that only you can provide.

Now, let's turn the page and face the great news ahead because, on the other side of your challenges lies your freedom. Whoever the Son sets free is free indeed.

CHAPTER 1

UNFIREABLE IN AN AI WORLD

In this season, a computer can draft emails, crunch numbers, cut videos, and answer customers in seconds. AI is not on the way; it is already here. Whole departments are getting "reorganized." Good people are going home with a severance check and a box of their belongings, wondering what just happened.

In the introduction, I told you the truth: AI is replacing jobs faster than many people can keep up, and in some industries, entire departments have been wiped out overnight. Folks with twenty years of service are hearing, "Your position is no longer needed." Their value didn't disappear. A system made a decision.

I need you to hear me clearly: AI can replace a position, but it cannot replace a purpose.

Your purpose is not written in code; it's written by God. Your calling is not stored on a server; it's carried in your spirit. Software can be upgraded. Your assignment cannot be canceled. You can be fired from your job, but you can never be fired from your purpose.

So the question is not, "Will AI change work?" It already has. The real question is, "How will you respond?" Will you freeze in fear or move by faith?

Will you allow technology to push you out of your lane, or will you learn how to make it work for the call on your life?

This chapter is about becoming unfireable in an AI world—not by running from it, but by understanding it, using it, and protecting the people most likely to be left behind.

Let's be honest. It's not just entry-level workers who are nervous right now. I've had C-suite leaders, pastors, nonprofit executives, and entrepreneurs pull me to the side and say, "Velma, I feel like I'm on borrowed time. I don't even understand this AI stuff they keep talking about."

If that's you, you are not crazy. You are not beyond help. But fear is not a strategy.

Ignoring AI will not save your job.

Pretending it doesn't exist won't stop your industry from changing. What will keep you anchored is purpose.

Your protection in an AI-driven world is not hiding from technology. Your protection lies in knowing why God put you here and then using every legal and ethical tool available—including AI—to multiply that assignment.

There has always been something "new" that scared people. There was a time when folks were nervous about the telephone, about the internet, and even about email. Every wave of change shook some people out and elevated others. The difference was never the technology. The difference was people's willingness to learn, adapt, and lead.

You are not called to be the one who is washed away by change. You are called to say, "Lord, show me how to use this for Your glory and for my assignment."

Let me tell you what happened when I first started paying attention to AI.

At first, I brushed it off. I was busy running companies, building programs, praying with people, and catching flights. I said what many people say: "That's for the tech folks." One day, I felt the Holy Spirit nudge me: "You keep asking Me to reach more people and do more in less time. What if some of the answer is in the tools you're ignoring?"

So I humbled myself and started experimenting. We didn't hand over our business to AI. We started small and strategic.

- We used AI to help us organize and outline training content for entrepreneurs, then I went back in and added the real meat—my testimony, my stories, my scripture, and my strategies.

- We used AI to summarize long reports and research so I could spend more time deciding and less time digging.

- We used AI to draft first versions of emails, social posts, and proposals, then my team edited them to sound like us and align with our values.

There was one project in particular where we had to build a new curriculum for a group of business owners in record time. In the past, it would have taken us months of late nights. With AI, we generated a skeleton in days. Then we did what only humans of purpose can do: we prayed, we edited, we added real examples and case studies, and we spoke life into those pages. Because of that, we were able to train more entrepreneurs, faster, with excellence... and several of them went on to win contracts, hire staff, and create jobs in their own communities.

AI took some of the hard work off our plates so we could show up fully in our assignment and in our communities. That's the picture I want you to see.

When I say "master AI," I am not talking about becoming a programmer. I'm talking about three simple commitments:

1. I will treat AI as a tool, not as a god or a monster. A hammer can build a house or break a window. It depends on the hands holding it. AI works the same way. It does not define your destiny. You decide how it's used in relation to your purpose.

2. I will delegate tasks to AI so I can focus on my assignment. You are too gifted to spend all your time formatting documents, writing the same email ten times, or copying notes from one place to another. If a tool can help you with that, let it. Free your mind and your schedule for the work only you can do—leading, building, praying, creating, and deciding.

3. I will use AI ethically. You don't use AI to lie, plagiarize, or pretend to be someone you're not. You use it to serve better, communicate more clearly, and show up stronger. You stay alert to bias. You ask, Who could this hurt? You pull your values into every decision.

Let's bring this concept to your desk, your laptop, and your phone. In any job or business, there are things an AI tool could do and things only you can do.

- Draft a first version of an email or proposal.
- Summarize notes from a long meeting.
- Help you brainstorm ideas or titles.
- Answer common questions.

Things AI cannot do:

- Carry the presence of God into that meeting.
- Build deep trust with a client, student, or team member.

- Discern when something looks profitable but will cost you your peace.
- Obey when God tells you to go left while everybody else is going right.

Being unfireable in an AI world means you intentionally move your time and energy away from what a tool can do and into what only your purpose can do.

Reflection Questions

- Where am I still doing work that a tool could handle?
- What do people come to me for that no computer can replace?
- How can I take one step this month toward using AI to clear space for my real assignment?

You are not here just to "hold a job." You are here to solve problems only you can solve.

A Word to Leaders and Institutions...

If you are leading a company, a university, a church, or a government agency, I want you to lean in. You cannot talk about innovation and ignore AI. But you also cannot talk about AI and ignore people.

If you rush to automate without educating, you are planting seeds of resentment and fear in your own house. If you implement AI with no plan to upskill the workers and small businesses around you, you are widening a gap you will eventually have to pay for.

But if you choose a different path—if you say, "We're going to teach, train, and lift while we innovate"—you can keep people who know your culture and your customers, help underserved entrepreneurs become tech-enabled suppliers instead of casualties, and build loyalty in a time when loyalty is rare.

That's what I help leaders do. I stand in the middle, between AI and access, between innovation and equity, and I help you build bridges so that when the future shows up, your people are ready for it.

You Are Still Unfireable

AI will keep changing. New tools will roll out. Some jobs will disappear. New roles will be created. That's the reality. But your purpose is not up for reorganization.

You can be fired from your job. You can be laid off. You can wake up one day and find your title is gone from the company website. What cannot be removed is what God put in you before the foundation of the world.

So lift your head. Learn what you need to learn. Use what you need to use. And walk in the confidence that while systems may shift, you, my friend, are unfireable.

If you are a leader who wants to build AI-ready, purpose-driven teams and supplier pipelines, my team and I design custom keynotes, executive briefings, and accelerator programs. Details are listed in the 'Work With Dr. Trayham' section in the back of this book.

CHAPTER 2

BORN INTO BATTLE: BREAKING GENERATIONAL CHAINS

I was born into a battle. This was not a physical war but a spiritual one. I came into this world fighting against generational curses, poverty, dysfunction, drug addiction, demonic restrictions, and cycles that awaited me before I ever took my first breath.

I was born to a fourteen-year-old mother in Houston, Texas, my hometown. I grew up in an environment where poverty was the norm, and escaping it felt impossible. I wasn't born with a silver spoon in my mouth; instead, I had to figure life out on my own without a proper example.

I was born on Easter, which earned me the family nickname "Bunny" or "Bunny Boo." Around nine years old, I was baptized and raised in a Baptist church. I remember singing in the choir and rehearsing my Easter speech. My grandmother, Mama Lynn, raised me, and I miss her deeply. She was a praying grandmother, and she prayed for me daily. Back then, I didn't really understand the power or significance of my grandmother's prayers.

It was a challenging upbringing. Every day was a struggle. There was little to no discussion about purpose, destiny, or the importance of solving problems;

it was more about simply trying to survive. I recall times when we had to visit community centers for Christmas toys or food banks for meals.

I did not understand that I had been born into a generational curse. Generational curses are not always about finances; they manifest in our thoughts, the fears we carry, the relationships we choose, and even the low standards we accept. For generations, my family had been trapped in cycles of poverty, lack, and demonic restrictions.

Yet, in the midst of all this, my grandmother remained steadfast in her prayers. I began to notice something change within me. What I didn't realize then was that even in that environment, my grandmother was planting seeds of hope and faith.

I eventually came to understand that my ending did not have to mirror my beginning. I decided to break free of these cycles. Although my grandmother couldn't provide me with money, she gave me something far more valuable: faith. Faith is the substance of things hoped for and the evidence of things not seen.

She covered me even when I didn't know what she was protecting me from. When I think about her prayers, I realize that they created a hedge of protection around me that no betrayal, failure, disappointment, or hijacking of destiny could break.

Eventually, I had to make a decision. At some point, I had to declare that my ending would not resemble my beginning. I'll say that again: my ending would not look like my beginning.

As you read this book, I want to ask you: how has your beginning influenced your perspective on your ending?

I began to believe God for something different. I started reading my Bible and came to understand the significance of baptism. I started to recognize the power in my grandmother's prayers.

I stopped viewing poverty as my lot in life and began seeing purpose as my birthright. I realized that I was born to solve a problem, that my very existence had a purpose.

What many people don't understand is that we all have spiritual gifts. A spiritual gift is an inherent capacity placed within us before we were born. Unfortunately, we often aren't taught about our spiritual gifts or how to solve problems. We aren't educated on how to "think and grow rich," which happens to be the title of one of my favorite books. I started to believe God for something different and to see myself as a solution to a problem.

My mother had me when she was just fourteen years old, and my biological father wasn't a part of my life. My stepfather did what he could to support us, but his efforts were not enough. He was, unfortunately, a factor in my mother's struggles with drugs from a very young age. Imagine growing up with a mother who was only fourteen when she had you.

However, it's not how you start; it's how you finish. Let me share a valuable lesson: We don't choose how we enter this world, but we do choose how we respond to our circumstances. You may have been born into brokenness, but you are not bound to repeat it. Born into poverty? Breaking free from it starts in your mind. Poverty is a state of mind.

My sense of purpose didn't begin when I started my first business; it began on the battlefield of my early life. Even the hardest situations can shape the leader within you. Your pain is part of the process.

Whatever you may be going through right now, remember this: life is 90 percent about how we respond to things and only 10 percent about what happens to us. Reflecting on my upbringing in poverty, with a young mother and a family that had very little, I can say that I am now a daughter of the Most High God. I am beautifully and wonderfully made. I am more than a conqueror.

You and I were born to solve problems, created with destiny and purpose within us.

When I consider the current economic and political climate, it's clear that we are all being called to solve problems. It's not how we start but how we finish that matters. I have read the Bible, one of my favorite books, more than six times, and one verse changed everything for me. This scripture serves as a blueprint for how I live my life: "For *I know the plans I have for you," declares the Lord, "plans to prosper you and not to harm you, plans to give you hope and a future" (Jeremiah 29:11).*

When I read this scripture, it anchors me. It reminds me that God didn't make a mistake and that even if people reject me or systems ignore me, He has a plan for my life.

I want to emphasize that this verse is a declaration from the Lord: *"For I know the plans I have for you."* These are plans to prosper you, not to harm you, but to give you hope and a future. Here's what I want you to understand: Breaking chains starts with faith. But what is faith? Hebrews 11 says that faith is the substance of the things we hope for and the evidence of things we do not see. However, faith must be accompanied by action. James 2 says that faith without works is dead.

To witness the manifestation of greatness and the plans that promise hope and a future, we must begin with faith and then take action. I want to tell you today that you do not need permission to break free from chains, shackles, generational poverty, limitations, or demonic restrictions. All you need to do is make a decision. You are equipped to win. Everything you need is already within you.

When I reflect on the atmosphere of limitations I experienced growing up, I think about the cycles of poverty and dysfunction in my family. These issues didn't start with my grandmother; they can be traced back through her mother and her mother's mother. Generations were impacted by poverty, dysfunction, alcohol abuse, dropping out of school, and a lack of education.

Poverty and dysfunction are not solely financial issues; they also manifest in our mindsets, our patterns, and the partners we choose. Therefore, breaking generational curses begins with faith and is sustained by action.

With that in mind, consider these reflection questions: What chains have tried to follow you into adulthood? Which generational curse are you determined to break in your family?

You were born into a battle, but you are equipped to win.

Let's go break some chains!

Let me share my thoughts about breaking generational curses. This process involves intentionally disrupting destructive cycles, whether they are mental, emotional, spiritual, relational, or financial. These are patterns that have repeated throughout our family lines. Breaking these curses is not just about what we leave behind; it's about what we create as we move forward.

In practical terms, the first step is to recognize these patterns. This begins with an honest examination of the cycles present in our families, such as:

- Constant poverty or financial mismanagement
- Abuse or toxic relationships
- Addiction, depression, or mental health stigma
- Inconsistent parenting, or what I refer to as "orphan syndrome"

I had to break free from my own experience with "orphan syndrome." My mother had me at age fourteen, and my father was not in my life, which left me feeling like an orphan.

These patterns also include settling for less, playing small, sabotaging yourself, having a victim mentality, and fearing success or failure.

One of my favorite quotes is, "You have to fail forward fast before you can reach your destiny."

Another prevalent pattern associated with generational curses is church trauma, spiritual manipulation, and a sense of abandonment in faith.

Breaking these curses begins with refusing to normalize the cycles we've repeated. We need to acknowledge that what we've endured does not define us.

The second step is to rewire our thinking. We must stop saying things like "That's just how I am," and "Nobody in our family has ever been a millionaire," or "No one in my life has ever overcome poverty." It's time to reframe our mindset. We need to stop accepting things as they are and recognize that while these issues may have been normal for us, they do not determine our destiny.

The phrase "It ran in my family until it ran into me" resonates with me because our words hold power over life and death. A scripture that has helped me during this journey is Romans 12:2, which encourages us to be transformed by the renewing of our minds. Curses begin to break when our thinking shifts.

We must renounce the lies and reclaim the truth. Spiritually, breaking a curse involves repenting from agreements, whether spoken or unspoken, with sin, fear, or failure. This means renouncing generational strongholds. For example, you can declare, "I break the spirit of poverty off my life in Jesus's name" or "I break the spirit of lack off my life in Jesus's name."

Lastly, we need to replace the lies we've believed with truth from Scripture and affirm our identity.

Here's an example:

I break the cycle of lack. I am a lender, not a borrower.

My family is blessed and will thrive for generations by doing what no one else has done. Breaking generational curses means taking decisive action.

I am starting a business to solve problems. I am healing family wounds through forgiveness and embracing change.

I choose to parent with grace rather than pain. I am learning about wealth, budgeting, boundaries, and belief. Curses are broken when someone commits to making different choices consistently.

Generational curses are fully broken when your children and their children walk in freedom. What does that look like? It means praying over your kids and their futures, just as my grandmother did for me.

It involves teaching them emotional intelligence and biblical truths from an early age, giving them the language for feelings and experiences. It's about helping them interpret their own truths.

Your children are created to solve problems, and by breaking a curse, you are also planting the seeds of a legacy. Breaking generational curses leads to a life free from financial poverty. This is the breakthrough action.

Declare this over yourself:

> *The generational cycle breaks with me. I will not repeat what I was born into. I am the first to be free, and whoever the Son sets free is free indeed. I am the interruption to dysfunction. I am the blueprint for breakthrough.*

CHAPTER 3

IT'S NOT HOW YOU START BUT HOW YOU FINISH

Let me say that again: It's not how you start but how you finish.

There's a lie that has been passed down through generations to underserved communities and to people of all ethnicities, both men and women, that suggests your past defines you, which is: if you have failed, then you are finished. That is absolutely untrue.

Temporary failure is not permanent defeat. I want you to understand the importance of finishing strong. It doesn't matter what you've gone through or who has hurt you, lied to you, or betrayed you; none of it matters.

What if I told you that success is not solely defined by your circumstances? Life is only 10 percent of what happens to us and 90 percent about how we respond. It's not how you start; it's how you finish. I know this personally because I didn't begin with wealth. I didn't start with privilege or resources. I didn't grow up with a father or a big family. I began in poverty, faced pain, and had my purpose buried under pressure.

But I made bold decisions, sometimes scary ones. Walking in faith can be frightening, but miracles don't occur without that leap of faith. Every decision I make is fueled by faith, reinforcing my belief that my end will not look like my beginning.

Let me share a story about one of my businesses, which was born from a necessity for freedom. Entrepreneurship was my chosen path. I've only had two jobs in my entire life: I worked for Google for nine months and then for a subrogation firm for a year and a half. I excelled at both jobs, but I realized that working for someone else wasn't my best path; I needed to pursue entrepreneurship if I was really going to get myself out of poverty.

One of my businesses was a luxury hair extension salon in Houston, Texas, called Jazzy Girls Luxury Hair Collection and Beauty Boutique. I opened this salon with no investors, just pure drive. I partnered with two luxury hair extension vendors, one from India and one from Brazil, to create a multicultural extension line. I hired top hairstylists, and the salon was located in the upscale River Oaks area of Houston. It was beautifully decorated in pink with stunning chandeliers, and I crafted a solid business model.

I conducted proper market research, hired the right staff, marketed my business effectively, and implemented the right systems. As a result, we created a brand that gained popularity among celebrities across the U.S., who began ordering products from Jazzy Girls Beauty Boutique.

Then one day, I was approached by a production team from the Animal Planet reality show *Call of the Wildman*. They came to my salon and said, "Wow, this is a beautiful salon! We would love to do a segment here. You're going to get millions of views!"

To me, this sounded amazing. I thought, *Wow, I have an opportunity to be on TV.* All of my hard work was finally paying off, and I felt like I was on the right track.

At that time, my salon was thriving, generating anywhere from $40,000 to $60,000 a month. It was an excellent business specializing in beautiful hair extensions. I had a multicultural blend of hair all on one wefting system, along with a product line called The Little Luxuries. This line featured eco-friendly shampoos and conditioners that people absolutely loved.

Returning to the Animal Planet situation, the production team came into my salon and was genuinely impressed. The show is typically filmed in the wild, with the focus on rescuing animals, so you might be wondering how that would translate to a hair salon. Nevertheless, the production team said, "Wow, this is amazing! We would love to help you gain more exposure," which was exciting; millions of viewers could be seeing my business.

Later that evening, I called my lawyer to share the fantastic news. I said, "Hey, we have a great opportunity! A production team from Animal Planet, an extremely well-known network, visited the salon today. They want to film a segment of their show *Call of the Wildman*, and we're going to get millions of views!"

To my surprise, my attorney replied, "Not so fast, Velma. You shouldn't do it."

I was taken aback. "What do you mean by 'not so fast'? This is a once-in-a-lifetime opportunity!"

She explained, "You don't know what they will actually film or the potential negative repercussions it might bring. I don't advise you to let your business be part of this reality TV show."

"But we'll get millions of views!" I argued.

"Velma, I truly don't think you should do it."

However, I decided to go ahead and do it anyway. I signed a non-compete and non-disclosure agreement, and since it's been almost eleven years, I feel it's okay to share this story.

I allowed them to film a segment for the show in my salon. (If you google "Jazzy Girls Bat Day Velma Trayham," you can find it. I love receipts.)

Here's the kicker: they planted bats in my salon. Yes, you read that right. They planted bats in my salon! The premise of the show was about rescuing these bats from my salon, which was part of the overall concept.

Then, the plot thickened: they accidentally left three bats for us to discover later. We found them dead, right outside the salon! I couldn't make this story up.

Then Mother Jones showed up. They are like the FBI for animals and wanted to interview the salon owner, and guess what? That salon owner was me! Yikes.

"Velma," my attorney said, "I told you not to do it. You signed an NDA, so you can't speak to them."

News stations, TV crews, and bloggers set up shop at the salon. Camerapeople set up multiple tripods outside, waiting to interview me. This situation lasted about three to four weeks, with various news outlets camped out in front of my salon.

Customers came by, saw the tripods, and took pictures to post on social media. They wondered, *What is happening at Texas Jazzy Girls?*

My attorney sighed and said again, "Velma, I told you not to do it, and you did it anyway."

What began as a $40,000- to $60,000-a-month operation slowly dwindled to zero in just three weeks after I accepted the invitation from Animal Planet to film in my salon. After about four weeks, I still couldn't conduct interviews, so the news networks began publishing whatever they wanted because I was unable to comment.

Ultimately, we had to close the brick-and-mortar business, which felt like a failure. However, I had a Canadian company interested in purchasing a large volume of our products. Ultimately, they purchased the Jazzy Girls business model for $250,000.

Publicly, many might see this story as a success since I sold my first business, but that's not the way I feel. This business could still be thriving today. I created solutions for women with medical-related hair issues, offering wigs and hair extensions. I was solving a real problem, and this failure felt personal.

Eventually, I realized that it wasn't the end; it was just the beginning. I learned that I needed to fail forward quickly before I could reach my true destiny. So let me spare you years of heartache by sharing this lesson.

When you trust people and seek their advice, it's important to truly listen to them and consider their guidance.

My early days with Jazzy Girls eventually led me to another venture. At that time, I was involved in fashion and opened a boutique, not because I felt a calling, but because I saw others doing it and thought, *Hmm, I can start a fashion business, too.* I tried to replicate someone else's concept, but it just didn't align with who I was.

Many people I encounter struggle with an identity crisis, often mimicking what others do instead of discovering what they are truly called to do. I wasn't operating in alignment with my purpose, which is why my business ultimately failed. It wasn't that fashion wasn't profitable; the business flopped because I wasn't meant for that field. I was acting out of necessity, driven by my upbringing in poverty.

Not every business is meant for everyone. Pursuing someone else's path can cause you to overlook the opportunities on your own. That was a difficult lesson for me—more money lost, but also more truths revealed.

Reflecting on my journey, I gained wisdom, insights, and valuable knowledge about building a successful company. I learned perseverance and how to apply these lessons to my future endeavors. While some family members and friends advised me to simply get another job, I felt strongly that I was meant to continue on this entrepreneurial path. I planned to apply everything I had learned to my next business, which I will discuss shortly.

However, I want to emphasize what failure taught me. Failure exposes what success often conceals. It reveals the truth about your mindset, habits, preparation, identity, and calling. Each failed business taught me lessons I needed to grow. Failure didn't mark the end for me; instead, it equipped me for the journey ahead.

I began to view loss not as defeat but as data. I learned what type of leader I wanted and needed to become. I discovered how to create systems and processes and to lead people effectively. I realized that entrepreneurship isn't solely about making money; it's about solving problems. When you focus on solving problems, you'll find that money follows solutions.

Entrepreneurship represents freedom. It's not just a career path; it's a declaration of independence. It means saying, "I will not be defined by my job title," and "I will not be confined by a system that doesn't value me." It's about building solutions that create impact and legacy. If more people understood this truth, millions would feel liberated.

You were placed on this earth to solve a problem. Each of us is born with the capacity to address a unique challenge. We all possess gifts, including spiritual ones—those inherent abilities instilled in us before birth.

You were created to be a problem solver. The greater the problem you address, the larger the impact and income you can generate. This isn't just business; it's purpose in action.

Failure became the lens through which I discovered the problem I was meant to solve. It's essential to understand that purpose isn't solely for entrepreneurs. Let me clarify that point.

You don't have to own a business to walk on purpose. Some of the most powerful change agents I've ever met weren't entrepreneurs; they were "intrapreneurs."

So, what is an intrapreneur? An intrapreneur is someone who leads from the inside out within public and private companies. They are the people transforming systems, shifting culture, solving problems, and sparking innovation within organizations. They are the team members who see injustice and speak up. They build new processes that serve more people, especially underserved communities. For example, it might be the woman in HR who rethinks hiring practices to reflect diversity and equity or the man in IT who simplifies systems to better support frontline workers.

Intrapreneurs don't wait for permission; they recognize problems and actively present solutions. The truth is, the world needs more intrapreneurs. The biggest companies in the world don't just need talent; they need purpose-driven leadership embedded at every level of their organization.

When I reflect on purpose-driven leadership and the current state of our country and economy, it's clear that Fortune 500 companies and other public companies are struggling to retain Gen Z, Gen Alpha, and millennial employees. Why? Because this demographic is seeking more purpose-driven leadership. It's not just about money; it's about having a sense of purpose in leadership.

Now let's discuss corporate allies.

I founded ThinkZilla Consulting as a marketing and public relations strategy firm. Initially, I aimed high. People often ask how I came up with the name ThinkZilla. To be honest, I wanted to name the company Godzilla, but since I couldn't trademark that name, I thought creatively and came up with ThinkZilla, home of big ideas and great results.

ThinkZilla started small; everything begins small. Rome wasn't built in a day, and neither were our cities or iconic airplane designs. When I first began ThinkZilla, I worked with pastors, many of whom weren't well known at the time, but my work helped elevate them to household names. I assisted some of the largest churches in our country in building community engagement programs.

Due to our success, we began receiving inquiries from government agencies and corporations seeking our help to build programs that support small businesses and underserved communities. This was amazing for me because, at the time, many smaller businesses couldn't afford our consulting services, yet I still wanted to help them grow. I wasn't quite sure how to achieve that initially.

However, as we gained attention, public and private companies approached us, eager to sign multi-year contracts to help them develop programs that would deliver resources to the community. We thrived in this space, assisting numerous government entities.

I realized that while many corporations wanted to make a difference, they often lacked the direction to do so. They had the budget but not the blueprint. They made numerous commitments to diversity, equity, and inclusion (DE&I) following the murder of George Floyd, which sparked widespread attention to these issues.

While many companies began to adopt the buzzword DE&I, ThinkZilla had already been doing the work long before it became a trending topic.

In my view, diversity, equity, and inclusion result from doing the right thing. When companies prioritize ethical practices, they naturally cultivate diversity. Unfortunately, many organizations formed DE&I committees without establishing genuine connections in the community. They launched PR campaigns but lacked the trust of the people they aimed to serve. That's when I realized that purpose not only transforms individuals but can also change entire companies.

Both public and private organizations play crucial roles in shifting societal norms, making corporate allies essential. Companies must go beyond merely writing checks; they need to commit to co-creation. This requires the humility to listen, the courage to restructure, and the innovation to develop solutions that truly benefit real people. They need purpose-driven consultants, faith-grounded advisors, and community builders.

And that is the mission of ThinkZilla. I created a culture focused on problem-solving, which led us to expand into cities such as Atlanta, Georgia; Miami, Florida; and Los Angeles, California. We even entered into a licensing agreement with a Canadian company under the ThinkZilla brand in Ontario, Canada. What began as a small marketing and public relations firm has evolved into an international community engagement organization that addresses some of the world's greatest challenges through public and private partnerships.

What does this mean for you? The world needs more purpose-driven consultants, faith-grounded advisors, and community builders, what I refer to as Nehemiah builders. The story of Nehemiah in the Bible illustrates the importance of determined problem solvers.

Whether you're an entrepreneur starting from scratch or someone reshaping legacy systems from within, you are a problem solver, and your purpose cannot be taken away from you. You might be let go from a job, but your purpose remains intact. You can transition out of a position or be underestimated in the boardroom, but if your assignment is rooted in purpose, it cannot be shut down by others.

ThinkZilla wasn't built overnight. It emerged from the lessons learned through my failures. I initially launched it as a marketing firm to assist high-impact leaders in expanding their reach, and then we began collaborating with corporations and government entities. As they expressed interest in reaching small businesses, I realized the gap between opportunity and access.

After experiencing failures at my first three companies, I recognized the disconnect: small businesses had potential but lacked capital, coaching, and capacity. On the other hand, corporations had resources but lacked connections to the community or the grassroots economy. It became clear to me that my mission was to bridge the two sides.

We developed curricula, tools, training programs, and mentorship opportunities, providing everything necessary to help people transition from poverty to purpose, from being overlooked to overcoming, and from merely surviving to thriving. What started as a simple idea has transformed into a national movement. I'm proud to say that I have helped thousands of entrepreneurs across the country rise above poverty.

We have created programs that fill the gaps where policy falls short, guiding people worldwide, both women and men, in shifting their mindset, structuring their businesses, and discovering their calling. And we are just getting started.

Reflection Questions:

- In what ways has failure served as a teacher rather than a conclusion for you? What lessons have you discovered in your losses?

- What problem are you uniquely positioned to solve? What challenges weigh on you but also inspire you? Are you an entrepreneur or an intrapreneur?

- How can you present yourself as a solution in your current environment?

Many people have asked me how I was steady in my conviction to keep going. Was it perseverance or faith?

I had faith and was determined to solve a problem. I knew I couldn't stop; I felt that if I didn't step up, then who would?

Having the opportunity to work at two different jobs, while also exploring entrepreneurship, made me realize there was a disconnect. Deep down, something within me wouldn't allow me to accept no as an answer.

I came to understand that if I was facing these challenges, countless others were likely dealing with the same issues. Purpose often arises from overcoming the obstacles that should have defeated us. The struggles I faced became my motivation. Now that I have conquered them, I possess the blueprint to help others navigate their challenges.

CHAPTER 4

LIVING YOUR PURPOSE: SOLVING THE PROBLEM YOU WERE BORN FOR

Let me be honest with you: I haven't always lived with the kind of peace I have now. I haven't always spoken on national stages or walked into rooms where kings and queens gather. I haven't always built and sold businesses or helped millions of people rise above poverty. There was a time when my life looked nothing like purpose; it looked like pain, poverty, and lack. It felt like hell on earth.

But something changed. It didn't happen overnight; it took time and obedience. And the shift didn't start with busyness; it started with purpose. Hear me when I say this: every choice is a seed, and every seed bears fruit.

You need to understand this truth if you want to live and lead with purpose. The peace I experience now is the harvest. The platforms I speak on now are part of that harvest. The people I get to serve are also part of the harvest. But it all started with intentional sowing. Before the influence, before the corporate contracts, and before the global reach, I was sowing in pain.

I was sowing in prayer. I was fasting. I was constantly sowing.

Here's the thing: we do not harvest in the same season we plant. So, if you're going through hell right now, in your business, with your family, in a relationship, or at your job, I urge you to begin sowing good seeds.

I was sowing in private, on my knees in prayer. I was crying out to God. I was going to revival services. There were weeks when I would spend twelve to thirteen hours in revival, crying out to God for change. I prayed, "God, change my life. Give me greater capacity. Strengthen me. Grant me spiritual eyes to see and ears to hear. Fight my battles for me. Show me what I need to know to fulfill my calling. Break generational curses and cycles in my family. Protect my children and me. Protect our nation. Raise up spiritual leaders who can disrupt corrupt systems."

I prayed and cried out, but I didn't see immediate changes. Sometimes, I didn't see anything for months. However, I began to realize this law of reaping and sowing: you don't get your harvest in the same season that you plant.

I encourage you to start sowing into God's kingdom on fertile ground. Three years ago, I initiated a weekly prayer call. Every Friday morning at 6:00 a.m., I host battle-ready prayer calls, and hundreds of people join each week. Many share testimonials about how the prayer call has changed their lives. Thousands of people have been covered in prayer, encouraged, and awakened. No matter where I am or what I am doing, that is my appointment with God to intercede for His people. Why? Because I believe that prayer is a seed.

I believe that every leader must first learn to support people spiritually before attempting to influence them in the physical realm. This is how I lead, how I build, and how I sow. Because of this approach, I have witnessed tangible impacts in my life, transforming from poverty to becoming a global businesswoman, from a place of need to one of purpose.

My beginnings did not provide me with a blueprint. I did not come from a background of wealth or a lineage of entrepreneurs; I came from a place of survival. I understand what it means to be broken in every way: mentally, financially, emotionally, and spiritually. I know what it feels like to be stuck, overlooked, and underestimated.

But I decided that my ending would not mirror my beginning. I began to sow seeds by investing in my learning. I focused on improving my mindset before addressing my financial situation. I prayed for leadership skills and the ability to guide God's people in the right way. That is what I prayed for.

I didn't pray for money, cars, or fame. I realized that dominion is not something we pursue; it is the result of our actions. Those were the seeds I sowed. I helped people start businesses and listened to their problems.

Now I am reaping the harvest because I sow seeds every day, whether through motivation, prayer, or conversations with my son and his football team. Every day, I look for opportunities to plant a seed.

Sowing seeds isn't always about financial contributions, but if you seek to grow in your financial capacity and prosperity, you need to sow. However, it's crucial to sow on fertile ground. Many people wonder why, despite tithing and attending the same church, their lives remain unchanged. I encourage you to pray and ask God if you are sowing on fertile ground. You don't necessarily need to sow into a church; you can invest in whatever helps you achieve your harvest.

Let me speak directly to my fellow businesswomen and corporate allies for a moment. I have built and sold companies, created national programs that have trained and impacted thousands of entrepreneurs, and consulted for cities, government agencies, and major corporations to bridge the gap between resources and real-life challenges. None of this happened by accident. It occurred because I stayed aligned with my assignment.

I stopped chasing money and instead focused on the problem I was born to solve. Let me ask you: Are you addressing the issue that God placed you on this earth to solve? Or are you merely clocking in, performing for praise, chasing numbers, pursuing superficial recognition, or hiding behind distractions?

You cannot be fired from your purpose. You may lose your job, but you can never be dismissed from your purpose. I am living proof of that. There were times I lost everything, times when people counted me out, times when doors closed right in front of me. There were moments when I didn't know how I would eat or move forward; my dreams felt delayed.

But God does not remove you from your assignment; He refines you for it. Every time I was pushed down, my purpose pulled me back up.

Heaven or hell, you get to choose. Many people believe that heaven and hell are just what happens after death. However, I'm here to tell you that you are either living in hell or heaven on earth right now.

Hell on earth is characterized by anxiety and fear. It binds you and makes you afraid.

Hell on earth includes negativity, surrounded by a circle of gossip. It means being constantly broke, despite your brilliance.

Hell on earth is being in a bad relationship that you know you need to leave. It's being in a job that doesn't value you. On the flip side, heaven on earth is the peace that surpasses your understanding.

Heaven on earth is having a purpose that awakens you with passion and zeal. It is the boldness to create what doesn't yet exist. Heaven on earth is about being an innovator, a trailblazer, a disruptor, or an entrepreneur who makes meaningful changes from the inside out.

Heaven on earth is the freedom to walk away from what doesn't align with your values. So, how do you create this heaven? It starts with the seeds that you sow.

I want to discuss what Scripture says about legacy. Proverbs 13:22 reads: *"A good person leaves an inheritance for their children's children."*

You are not just called to exist; you are called to break chains and build systems that your grandchildren will benefit from.

Jeremiah 29:11 states, *"'For I know the plans I have for you,' declares the Lord, 'plans to prosper you and not to harm you, plans to give you hope and a future.'"* This means God's plan for you includes provision, prosperity, community, and purpose, but it also requires partnerships. God won't force you to sow; He gives you the seed, and it is up to you to plant it and know where to sow it.

Recently, I spoke with a young woman who was contemplating suicide. She shared that she didn't want to live anymore. At one time, she had been a corporate leader who had climbed to the top of her field, but recent economic and political shifts had led to her losing her job. She had exhausted her savings and hit rock bottom.

I asked her about the seeds she had sown during her time in the corporate world. How had she helped build community? What types of change had she facilitated? I posed these questions because I wanted to understand why life had hit her so hard. While I'm not suggesting this is the sole reason, there is a law of reaping and sowing.

When I asked her how many times she had fed the homeless, provided clothing to those in need, offered shelter, or prayed for others, she admitted the answer was none. I told her, "My sister in Christ, you need to start sowing seeds now to see a harvest in the next season." I also warned her that things might get worse before they get better, as she was reaping what she had sown, and currently, she hadn't sown any seeds.

You need to choose obedience over self-interest. Choose to help others, save souls, and feed the hungry. Use your mind, influence, and capacity to advance God's kingdom on earth as it is in heaven. When you focus on solving problems, you will find that money follows solutions.

That is why I felt compelled to write this book. You can be fired from your job, but you can never be fired from your purpose. If you're ready to stop living in lack and fear or being bound by generational curses and cycles, if you're ready to stop living in mediocrity, here's what I will ask of you:

Identify the problem, offer a solution, and operate in excellence. Find a problem to solve in this world. Provide a solution tailored to a specific demographic or niche audience, and strive for excellence in your approach.

This path has taken me from barely surviving to receiving invitations from the White House, from being a single mother's daughter to becoming a national and international leader. If God did it for me, He can do it for you. So, make a conscious choice to live powerfully.

The life I lead today didn't come without a cost. It was achieved through tears, trials, and seasons of silence, but I wouldn't trade it for anything. Remember, there's isolation before elevation.

When you truly walk in your purpose, you're not just alive; you're free. The Bible tells us that whoever the Son sets free is free indeed. So, I'll leave you with this thought:

You can lose your title or your paycheck, but when you're solving the problem God assigned to you, that can never be taken away.

So, build wisely, act boldly, and live as if you're living in heaven on earth because, when you're in your purpose, it truly is.

Reflection Questions:

- What seeds are you sowing in this season? Are they aligned with your purpose or merely with self-promotion?

- Are you solving the problem you were born to address, or are you chasing someone else's assignment?

- How have your past choices shaped the results you are experiencing now?

- What needs to change so you can build a legacy that your children's children can inherit?

When I moved from my hometown of Houston, Texas, to Atlanta, I stepped out in faith. I left my family behind to start a new life and figure things out.

During the first forty days in Atlanta, I completely disconnected from distractions. I didn't watch TV, use social media, or read magazines. Instead, I dedicated that time to prayer and fasting, seeking guidance from God. I asked Him to help me unlearn everything I had been taught and to rewire my thinking. I recognized that my life didn't belong to me but to Him, and I needed divine assistance in this process.

During this time of introspection and growth, I began unlearning beliefs and attitudes that I had held for years. I developed a deeper interest in understanding people from all walks of life, their backgrounds, cultures, and perspectives. I came to appreciate the fact that, although we are all different, we share common desires: to be loved, to be successful, and to provide for our families.

I realized that we all bleed the same and have similar aspirations. As I unlearned those old ways of thinking, my heart grew for God's people. I understood that people prefer to do business with those they know, like, and trust; authenticity is crucial.

I committed to being the authentic version of myself rather than a cheap imitation of anyone else, and that decision led to a significant transformation in my life.

CHAPTER 5

WHEN GOD SAYS GO: YOUR REBIRTH

Eventually, I knew it was time to leave my hometown, Houston, Texas. After going through a divorce, I felt that when you have nothing to lose, you have everything to gain.

I authored a book titled *When God Says Go* in 2017, and I initially intended to write a sequel. One day, I probably will. However, the Lord impressed upon my heart that *When God Says Go* was a rebirth, a journey toward walking in my true purpose and destiny.

After my divorce, I moved to Atlanta, Georgia. It was truly a faith journey. Faith is the substance of things hoped for, the evidence of things not seen. I ventured to Atlanta to start anew, feeling like I had lost nearly everything.

My divorce was difficult. Although my ex-husband and I had built multiple businesses together, I told the judge I didn't want anything from him. All I wanted at that time was peace. We had multiple cars, various businesses, and a lot of material possessions, but I realized that, at that stage in my life, what I truly desired was inner peace.

So, I moved to Atlanta.

I understand what it means to feel broken. I know what it feels like to hit a wall that seems insurmountable. I was involved in a car crash that, by all earthly standards, should have ended my life, but it didn't.

I will never forget that moment. My son, King Mauni, was five years old when we left Houston, and it took me some time to find a daycare for him before I could figure out my next steps in Atlanta. I still had my consulting business at the time, had expanded it into Atlanta, and had started a nonprofit called Millionaire Mastermind Academy, which aims to end poverty through entrepreneurship.

During this time of rebirth, I thought my life was over. There was a moment when it seemed that life could, and by all accounts, should have ended for me. But when God says go, everything changes. I encourage anyone who hasn't read *When God Says Go* to do so; it's a powerful testament to personal struggle and growth.

This chapter is not about theology; it focuses on purpose-driven leadership and how we often must experience a spiritual death to live. True leadership doesn't begin with a title; it begins with your impact on the world for a greater good. My true leadership journey began at the car crash.

I vividly remember the first day I enrolled my son in a performing arts school in Atlanta. The day I had the crash was his first day there. I was on my way to a meeting that I shouldn't have been taking.

A couple of weeks before the car crash, my spiritual father called me. He told me he sensed that the enemy was trying to take me out and that my life was in danger, along with a potential disruption of my kingdom's purpose. At the time, I wasn't sure what that meant.

He began to pray for me. This was just two weeks before the accident. In fact, he even wrote the foreword to *When God Says Go,* in which he shared that the Lord advised him to reach out to me because he had seen in the spirit that I was in danger.

I remember that day like yesterday. It was the first day my son attended Tayo Reed's Performing Arts School in Atlanta. He was a five-year-old tap dancer. Fast forward to now, and he's fourteen years old, a star football player as a freshman. He's playing varsity, and now he's taller than me. Who would have imagined that the little kid who was tap dancing would become the second fastest boy in his age group in the state of Arizona?

Now, back to the story. I am incredibly grateful that I enrolled him in school. If he had been with me that day, I don't know what might have happened.

This is the crash that changed everything. I was en route to that meeting I shouldn't have been attending. I was on the phone and eating chicken, not really paying attention to the road, when I was struck by a semi-tractor truck, which spun my car around in the middle of traffic. Then another truck hit me.

The car was totaled. A luxury model, it had all the safety features, yet not a single airbag deployed during the crash. I was spun around in traffic, and the airbags still did not deploy. When the car finally came to a rest, all I remember is hearing people screaming, "Is she alive?"

I was taken to the hospital by Life Flight, and when I woke up, the doctor said, "I don't know how you survived this car crash, but you don't even have a scratch on you." At that moment, I realized that sometimes you have to die spiritually to live physically.

I had a revelation: *God, if you spared me, it's because I'm not done yet.* It was more than just survival; it was my rebirth. What I want to share with you is that there is still purpose and destiny for your life. Many people did not wake up this morning, but the fact that you are alive and reading this means you've probably been praying for signs.

Consider the fact that you are reading this book as your sign. God did not just save my life from that accident; He was calling me out of what was wrecking me, which was my comfort zone. I'll say that again: God didn't just rescue me from a wreck; He was calling me out of what was wrecking me.

Miracles happen in the unfamiliar; they occur when we step out in faith. When I think about the incredible stories in the Bible, I think of Noah building an ark before it was needed. People thought he was crazy for doing so.

Jesus started his ministry in Nazareth, his hometown, where he faced rejection. People questioned him, asking, "Isn't this the carpenter's son? Isn't he Mary's son? Who does he think he is?" He then moved to Capernaum, where people believed in him, and that's where the miracles began. This contrast isn't just biblical; it's practical. Nazareth represented comfort, familiarity, and doubt, while Capernaum embodied expectation, openness, and breakthrough.

Your purpose often lies in the unfamiliar, but you can't reach it without leaving what is familiar behind. I think about leaving Houston, my hometown, as being similar to how Jesus left Nazareth. If I hadn't left, I couldn't have performed the miracles I'm now part of, though I'd say God is working through me.

Many lives have been transformed; thousands of entrepreneurs now experience financial freedom thanks to programs I've developed to combat poverty through entrepreneurship. Thousands have started small businesses, and millions have interacted with my teachings. Over a million copies of my book *When God Says Go* have been sold through speaking engagements and bulk sales.

I believe that when we understand the importance of leaving the familiar behind, we can step into the unfamiliar, where breakthroughs occur. It's important to perform a "Nazareth inventory" and ask yourself, *What environment is hindering your purpose? Who are the people whose approval I overvalue? What is God calling me to walk away from? What does He want me to stop?*

Your next level of purpose won't be birthed from familiarity. It requires obedience, boldness, and stepping beyond the safe lines you've drawn. Sometimes, obedience means leaving what feels familiar, even if you think it's not broken.

Often, we believe we're winning when, in reality, we are losing. Conversely, we may think we are losing when we are actually winning. After my car crash, I felt like I was losing. I had gone through a divorce and left everything behind. The enemy seemed to be trying to take me out, and my only car was totaled. I found myself wondering what my purpose was.

On the surface, it might have appeared as though I was doing well, but even when we think things aren't broken, that can be misleading. Many people feel they have arrived at their destination, judging success by titles, job positions, or accolades. However, I'm here to tell you that we have not truly arrived. Why? Because there are souls to save, problems to solve, and homelessness that needs addressing. Additionally, we must focus on mental health issues happening around the world and give the next generation a blueprint to follow.

If you think you've reached your destination, you haven't. When I reflect on my purpose and destiny, specifically my mission to end poverty through entrepreneurship, I never had a clear plan for how to achieve it. When I felt like I was losing, I was actually winning because I stayed focused on the unknown and the unfamiliar.

I kept walking in faith, continually asking myself, *what's the worst that could happen?* After all, you can't miss what you never had.

Nazareth was home to Jesus, but it was also a place where miracles were limited by familiarity. Just like Jesus, I had to leave my hometown to find my own Capernaum, a place of miracles, momentum, and manifestation. That's what I released when God said, *"Go."* It was raw, it was real, and it was everything I was too ashamed to share out loud, yet I knew it had to be written. People didn't know my story before I accepted God's call.

I was afraid and embarrassed to admit that my mother struggled with addiction and that my father was absent. It was painful. So, this journey became not only a rebirth but also a declaration: I would no longer let my beginnings define me. It's not how you start; it's how you finish. I realized I would no longer apologize for being called to fulfill my purpose.

Many are called, but only a few are chosen. Are you one of God's chosen ones for such a time as this? I proudly share that over a million copies of *When God Says Go* have been sold, not because of me, but because of what God wanted to accomplish through me.

What began as a book evolved into a pillar of support for thousands, even millions, to find courage in their calling. This book is no different. You may be fired from your job, but you can never be dismissed from your purpose.

Here's what I've learned and shared in boardrooms, prayer calls, economic empowerment speeches, and universities and high schools across the world: obedience is better than sacrifice.

Obedience unlocks overflow. Miracles occur in the unfamiliar. Faith is the substance of things hoped for and the evidence of things not seen.

True leadership starts the moment you walk away from who the world expects you to be and move toward who God created you to be. You are not just here to exist; you are here to lead.

You're here to solve a problem, and that begins with being attentive to the moment when God says, *"Go."* Let me clarify: I'm not preaching or presenting this as a religious text, but I want to illustrate a principle of purpose-driven leadership.

In Nazareth, Jesus faced doubt; in Capernaum, He was welcomed. You cannot thrive in an environment where people are committed to misunderstanding your identity.

This is why your roots matter, both spiritually and professionally. Where you're planted influences what you can produce.

If you're in an environment where your gifts are minimized, your voice is silenced, and your purpose cannot shine, your calling will be limited. When I left Houston for Atlanta, went through a car crash, and surrendered my life to God, saying, "Not my will, but Your will be done," things changed. Doors opened without me even knocking. God was waiting for my movement to release my miracle.

Too often, we think we need to know the end from the beginning, but God will never reveal the whole path upfront. Many people focus on having a strategy, but I know plenty of individuals with strategies who remain stuck. God is waiting for you to embrace your moment to move forward.

Let's get practical for a moment. I've developed what I call the **Rebirth Leadership Model**, which I'll outline later in this chapter. It is built around five key shifts: **Catalyst, Calling, Courage, Clarity, and Capacity.**

1. *Catalyst* is the crisis, loss, or revelation that shakes your identity and exposes what is no longer working.

2. *Calling* is the inner conviction that rises up in that disruption and lets you know you cannot stay where you are.

3. *Courage* is the bold, often uncomfortable move you take toward the unknown in response to that calling.

4. *Clarity* is the sharpening of your vision and direction as you obey step by step.

5. *Capacity* is the increase in your influence, abilities, and peace that God produces in you as you walk out that vision over time.

This model isn't based on theory; it's drawn from my life experiences. I reached a point where my own Catalyst hit—I had truly come to the end of myself, exhausted, frustrated, and, as I often say, "sick and tired of being sick and tired." That breaking point was the Catalyst and became the doorway to Calling, Courage, Clarity, and eventually a new level of Capacity in my leadership and purpose.

I used to tell people that I had come to the very end of myself. What I mean by that is I was sick and tired of being sick and tired.

I was exhausted from feeling like I wasn't operating on my purpose. It felt as though I was letting the world use me without getting anything in return. I realized that if I allowed the world to use me, and if my family allowed the world to use them, it was no wonder we were in poverty. Breaking generational curses and cycles is important because someone has to take the first step.

Having a family history filled with poverty, drug addiction, demonic restrictions, alcohol abuse, and a lack of education, I understood what poverty breeds. I began to ask myself, *What's the worst that can happen?* This fueled my determination to keep fighting. I was truly sick and tired of being sick and tired, so I began to cry out.

I prayed to God, asking Him to change me, to rewire my brain, and to allow me to unlearn the things I had learned. I wanted to function in alignment with heaven's plans. The Lord's word in Jeremiah 29:11 assures us, *"For I know the plans I have for you, declares the Lord, plans to prosper you and not to harm you, plans to give you hope and a future."* If that is the promise God has made about us, then I had to wonder why people weren't seeing that promise come to pass.

I realized it doesn't happen overnight. For a prophecy or a declaration to manifest, you must go through a season of processing, pruning, and consecration to reach the other side.

Another scripture that profoundly impacted me is 2 Chronicles 7:14, which states, *"If my people, who are called by my name, will humble themselves, turn from their wicked ways, and cry out to me, then I will hear from them and will heal their land."*

This made me pause. It suggests that many people are praying, but heaven might not be hearing them because they have not embraced humility and turned away from wickedness. This understanding led me to recognize that I needed to walk the right path.

None of us will be perfect, as perfection doesn't exist, but I realized I had to make an intentional effort to choose the right path so that my children and my children's children would not have to endure what I went through.

Every new level of growth requires a new level of revelation.

We can only see from our current spiritual level, and each new level demands greater capacity and deeper intimacy with God. Most people don't advance to the next level because they remain at the same spiritual stage.

With every new level and season, my clarity, focus, and purpose have grown. It's almost like adding pieces to a puzzle. Things I did in the previous season, connections I made, or experiences I had didn't seem significant at the time. But now, in this season, I see how they contribute to something great.

The Bible tells us to *"seek ye first the kingdom of heaven and everything else will be added unto us"* (Matthew 6:33). Therefore, my purpose is still unfolding, as I have received the instruction to write this book.

I know this instruction comes from heaven because I'm incredibly busy right now; this is the busiest time of the year for me, but the Holy Spirit prompted me to start writing the book regardless. I prayed and said, "Okay, God, I'll do it. But who will help me? Who will be the publisher?"

I had met some publishers before, but I didn't feel good about those options. I thought, *Lord, if I have to work with this person, I might as well wait for you to send the right one.* Then I met Paul in a very unexpected way.

Paul, along with his wife, family, and colleagues, came to Arizona and reached out to me to do a podcast. I thought, *Why would I travel to Florida for a podcast?* The only time I feel compelled to go is when God says, "Go." But so much has happened since that moment.

Then I learned about the Black Chamber of Arizona. Many people don't understand what a chamber does, but that felt like confirmation number two for me. After that, I read Alex's book and thought, *Wow, I like this.* Alex then invited me to speak at one of his events.

I told Alex, "I appreciate the invitation, but I don't have a call to action right now, and I don't feel comfortable speaking without one." I'm used to speaking in my areas of expertise to government officials, banks, and the boards I serve on because it relates to my work with the chamber and my nonprofit. However, speaking to a room full of entrepreneurs who need insight relevant to the message of this book felt different.

That was another confirmation for me. Alex then connected me with Chris, and I took some time to pray about it. For a few weeks, I sought clarity because the Bible teaches that while man's plans can fail, God's plans will succeed. I wanted to ensure that everything I did was aligned with His will.

When I finally met Chris, although the costs were higher than my previous options, I found peace with it. The Lord affirmed my decision, and from that point, I knew it was time to move forward.

For the past three and a half years, I have been fasting every Monday from 6 a.m. to 6 p.m. I also hold prayer calls every Friday at 6 a.m., which hundreds of people join. Today, during my fast, I reflected on the fact that we've scheduled the recordings for this book on Mondays, my fasting days.

Coincidentally, we didn't plan to record on Mondays; it just happened that way. During my fast, I don't eat anything from 6 a.m. to 6 p.m. I pay attention to these details because I feel connected to the frequency of heaven through my obedience.

To date, I have built and sold several companies. I was honored with a White House Lifetime Achievement Award for helping thousands of entrepreneurs rise above poverty. I have spoken on both national and international stages and have led government initiatives.

I have been featured in *Forbes* and *Black Enterprise* and recognized as one of the Most Influential Women in Arizona and one of the Top 100 Women to Know in America by JPMorgan Chase. However, what I am most proud of is that, for the past three years, I have hosted a battle-ready prayer call every Friday morning, rain or shine, whether I'm at an airport, a hotel, in America, or abroad. I never miss it.

Why? Because true leadership begins in the spirit before it manifests in reality. I have invested in the lives of millions, and I continue to do so. Sometimes, I do this with a microphone, sometimes with a message, and sometimes with financial support, but I always do it with my faith.

For the corporate leaders reading this, this is not just motivation; it is transformation. This is an impartation that will lead to true change. The world is evolving. Consumers desire authenticity, employees seek meaning, and stakeholders demand integrity. The most powerful companies will be led by those who understand that purpose drives the bottom line and that obedience leads to innovation.

Rebirth is not about religion; it is about strategy. Rather than a setback, it is a setup for a comeback.

I am no longer who I used to be, and I thank God for that. I am no longer leading from survival; I am leading from a place of significance, abundance, and the prosperity that God promised me. When God said, *"Go,"* I said, "Yes," and I have been walking in peace and purpose ever since.

When you step out in faith, heaven steps in with power.

CHAPTER 6

BECOMING A FIREBRAND

Let me start by saying this: you were not created to remain silent, shrink yourself, or conform to broken systems. You were never meant to blend in; you were called to shine brightly.

Born to be a firebrand, a leader, a changer of atmospheres, and a disruptor of the kingdom, you are part of a vital mission. The Kingdom of God operates through structures, and He is working to dismantle those demonic, systemic structures that hell has established.

Not everyone is called to be a firebrand, and not everyone will understand your passion. That's because they are not meant to carry what you possess.

Let me share a story that ignited my journey to becoming a firebrand. In the winter of 2018, when the federal government shut down, a wave of panic swept through our nation. People lost their jobs, their income stopped, and hope began to fade.

At that moment, I realized this issue extended beyond politics. It was about poverty and purpose. It was about a woman who has more vision than access. I remember sitting in my room, praying and asking God what I should do with the insights and wisdom He had given me, as well as the gift of discernment I possessed.

One of my greatest spiritual gifts is discernment. If we are not discerning during these challenging times, we are in trouble. Some may wonder, what is discernment?

Discernment is the ability to make wise decisions, especially in complex and challenging situations. In a Christian context, spiritual discernment involves distinguishing between God's will and the will of hell.

Now, let's briefly discuss spiritual warfare. Many people ask, "What is spiritual warfare?" The term refers to a power struggle between the Kingdom of Heaven and the kingdom of darkness. The Kingdom of Heaven is calling out to you, just as the kingdom of darkness is.

When I prayed to God, His answer came quickly and decisively: create a space where women can rise. This is how the vision for the Millionaire Mastermind Academy was born.

I founded the Millionaire Mastermind Academy in 2018 as a nonprofit organization with the mission to end poverty through entrepreneurship for women worldwide. I organized the first economic empowerment event, starting with just a few dozen women and growing to thousands. Initially, I had no budget, no fancy names, no celebrity talent, nothing but my commitment to obedience.

At the first event, thirty women showed up, and what happened in that room sparked a fire that would never be extinguished. I witnessed single mothers crying because they felt hope for the first time. One woman shared that she had been planning to end her life the following week but now had something to live for.

I felt the immediate impact of what was happening; it was a powerful moment. I didn't know how everything would unfold, but I understood the importance of being obedient, especially after hearing so many inspiring stories.

As time passed, the momentum grew. Women began flying in from all over the country to attend these economic empowerment events. They thought they were coming to hear me speak, but they were actually seeking to witness what faith looked like. They wanted to discover their purpose and learn how to walk in faith and carry the fire that many said I possessed. I still hear that today: "You carry a fire, Dr. Trayham, like none other."

Fast forward to today, and thousands of women, including corporate leaders, government officials, solopreneurs, and entrepreneurs, have benefited from the seeds sown back in 2018.

Leadership is crucial because many people pray for various things. However, God often only provides what we are capable of leading and managing effectively. Leadership isn't about control; it's about serving others.

It's about walking on purpose and helping others do the same. It's about solving problems. A real leader doesn't just guide; they ignite.

That's what becoming a firebrand is all about. It's not comfortable. We must unlearn the lies that have kept us small and step boldly into a purpose that shakes systems and dismantles structures established by oppression.

Poverty is a state of mind. It's not just a lack of money; it's a lack of vision because, as the Bible tells us, where there is no vision, the people perish.

Poverty reflects a lack of mindset, access, creativity, and problem-solving abilities. When you become a firebrand, you don't just change your life; you also become a thermostat for others.

That is what being a firebrand means. When you have that fire because you are solving problems, you begin to feel a sense of zeal and energy. I tell people all the time, "I am zealous." I show great energy and enthusiasm at all times. Am I perfect? No, but this mindset has become part of how God has rewired my brain.

The 2018 government shutdown was a disruption that demanded reinvention. Then, in 2020, COVID-19 hit, shutting down everything but not purpose.

I decided to survey the thousands of women who had attended an economic empowerment event, and I received hundreds of replies. The stories were heartbreaking, revealing that COVID-19 had led many to lose their jobs, homes, and businesses. People were struggling to feed their children and grappling with identity loss, yet they still attended economic empowerment events that we moved to a virtual platform. They thought, *If God did it for Dr. Trayham, maybe He can do it for me, too.*

From the survey, I found that many women in corporate roles felt tired of being part of a puzzle. They sensed they weren't walking in their purpose and destiny, and they desired more. So, I created digital curricula, leadership tracks, and mentorship cohorts. I built virtual stages where women could still be empowered.

Most people would call that a strategy; I call it spiritual engineering. Many lives have been transformed.

Here's what I've learned from the challenges of the government shutdown in 2018 and COVID-19, when many were suffering greatly. To be a firebrand, you must be willing to do three things:

1. **Carry the fire even when no one is clapping.** This means you keep showing up with excellence, passion, and obedience even when there is no audience, no applause, and no visible reward. You choose to

honor your assignment in the dark so that when the lights come on, your character is already prepared for the stage.

2. **Share your testimony even when you think no one is listening.** When I think about the New Testament, it's filled with testimonies of Jesus Christ. Though there have been arguments about His divinity, there has never been a denial of the miracles He performed, as recounted by Matthew, Mark, Luke, and John.

Research shows that the Gospel writers were sharing what they experienced firsthand. They were eyewitnesses who documented their experiences and preserved those accounts in a metaphorical treasure chest, not knowing they would later become part of the New Testament.

They were simply documenting what they witnessed. In the same way, it is the power of your testimony that can set a nation free. My own testimony is why you are reading this book today. It has enabled thousands of people to overcome poverty. This is what it means to be a firebrand: refuse to dim your light for environments that weren't designed for your brilliance.

3. **Always reignite and empower others.** Remember, life and death are in the power of the tongue. Whatever a person speaks is what they become. I have experienced doubts and sad days, moments where I felt lost and uncertain. However, I have learned to dismiss the voice of defeat and consistently rise in purpose. Every single day, I must die to my flesh, to fear, doubt, oppression, and depression. I have to rebuke these negative feelings and declare what I want my life to look like.

You don't become a firebrand by accident, just as success is not a matter of luck. You become a firebrand when you decide you will no longer play small to protect weak systems. You will no longer simply check a box or think highly of yourself because of your title. You become a firebrand when you fully commit to walking with purpose.

One of my favorite quotes is, *"We are born looking like our parents, but we die looking like our decisions."* Do you have the desire to become a firebrand, no matter the cost? Do you want to change the world? Do you wish to create a foundation that ensures your children's children have a blueprint to follow after you're gone? You become a firebrand when you take your mission seriously.

Over the years, the reach of the Millionaire Mastermind Academy has helped more than eight thousand entrepreneurs. Many of these business owners have launched sustainable enterprises, purchased homes, created jobs, and broken generational cycles.

What started in obedience has turned into a nationwide movement. I share this not to brag but to inspire you to break free from the limitations you've been living in. When you say yes to your purpose, the world takes notice. We are now collaborating with corporations, government agencies, large banks, and private foundations because firebrands don't just shift rooms; we shift nations.

True purpose-driven leadership isn't about the title; it's about transformation. It's about seeing the bigger picture and having the courage to say, "I don't need your permission to lead. I have a divine assignment to fulfill." This is how we build influence with impact. Dominion is not something you pursue; it is the result of your actions.

It's not simply about climbing ladders but about building legacies. It's not just about speaking on stages; it's about speaking life into systems and dismantling the structures that negativity has established.

I want to share a quick story about when I launched the Millionaire Mastermind Academy. There was a time when I considered giving up. After a few years, I had invested nearly a million dollars into the nonprofit, empowering women, hosting events, and creating programs. I found myself thinking, *Lord, I want to continue this, but I don't have the financial means to go on.*

Then, I received a $500 donation, which came just a week after I prayed. Curious about the sender, I looked up the name associated with it: Joe Lubeck. I soon discovered that he is the president and CEO of American Landmark Apartments, one of the fastest-growing multifamily property owners in the country, with billions of dollars in assets. I was intrigued and reached out to him to express my gratitude for the donation.

"Thank you for this support; it's the first donation I've received," I said. I felt a wave of encouragement wash over me like a "faith bomb." Joe Lubeck responded that he had been following the work I was doing with women in our community and wanted to help further.

He asked, "What do you need?" At the time, I was looking to launch the first entrepreneur accelerator program and needed $50,000, not only to start it but also to provide grants. I shared my vision with Joe, and he said, "We will send you the check."

They sent the check, and the first accelerator program was a success. I fulfilled every promise I

The subsequent events unfolded as history. That initial $500 donation, followed by the $50,000, attracted attention from large banks, municipalities, and corporations eager to support the Millionaire Mastermind Academy. I prayed, and God answered. Someone showed up to help.

Joe Lubeck, who has a wonderful family and a lovely wife, has now been on the board of the Millionaire Mastermind Academy for two years.

I want to emphasize that when you walk in your purpose, everything else falls into place. When you take a step forward, God aligns heaven's resources with your actions. Faith is the substance of things hoped for and the evidence of things not seen.

Today, more than eight thousand entrepreneurs have completed our program.

Now, I want to pause for some reflection with a self-assessment exercise. Here's a quick quiz: Rate yourself on a scale from one to ten regarding your passion for purpose, your conviction to speak the truth, your willingness to stand out, your consistency in public and private institutions, and your courage to lead even when no one is applauding.

Then ask yourself: What message are you still afraid to express out loud? What part of yourself are you hiding instead of leading? Who needs your courage right now? Who needs you to be bold?

When I think of leaders like Harriet Tubman, Martin Luther King Jr., and Jesus Christ, one commonality stands out: they weren't loved by the systems of their time but by the people. They refused to conform to man-made limitations, sparking revolutions that resonate even today.

You are no different. Your obedience may be misunderstood, and your passion might be feared. However, remember that playing small does not make the world safer; it makes it sadder.

Let me speak directly to you: You were not called to blend in. You were called to shine brightly. You are the fire; you are the catalyst for change. You are the person generations have been waiting for. Now, go and set the world ablaze.

Write down one thing you've been afraid to do. Then write a date to act on it.

Share your truth on social media or with a trusted community. Share your testimony. Take one bold step this week toward a firebrand life.

CHAPTER 7

A MESSAGE FOR THE WEALTHY

What you sow in faith, you reap in purpose. I want to speak directly to those who have been blessed with wealth, influence, networks, and opportunities.

This chapter is a call to stewardship, legacy, and purpose. Let me begin by sharing how one man's $500 seed became a harvest that touched thousands of lives and how that small act of generosity opened the door to transformation across America.

In the previous chapter, I shared the story of how a $500 seed from Joe Lubeck came at the exact moment I was ready to give up on the Millionaire Mastermind Academy. That single act of generosity helped launch our first entrepreneur accelerator program and ultimately impacted thousands of lives. But that story isn't just about my journey. It's about the power of stewardship.

Joe is one of my favorite people in the world. He had been observing my work and its impact from afar.

When I received his donation, I immediately began researching Joe so I could thank him properly. I looked him up on LinkedIn and discovered that he wasn't just a donor; Joe was a billionaire, a real estate investor, and a philanthropist. This wasn't merely about the $500; it was about divine timing.

It was as if God were saying, "Don't you dare quit. The right people are watching. You don't harvest in the same season that you plant."

Within days of receiving the donation, Joe and I had the opportunity to speak. I thanked him for his generosity, and he replied, "I want to do more. I want to sow seeds. I want to teach women, especially single mothers. I want to help Black women and aspiring entrepreneurs. I want to help them learn how to fish. I want to partner with you. What do you need from me?"

I told him about an entrepreneur program I had created, which included a fully developed curriculum, and expressed my desire to help women entrepreneurs complete the program and to award six women $5,000 grants to fund their startups. To run this six-month program, I needed $50,000. The program consisted of weekly sessions focused on entrepreneurship, building contracting capacity, developing a mission and vision, developing a solid revenue model, and understanding the target audience.

I named my curriculum "Plan, Start, and Build a Successful Company," but I called it the "Pioneer Curriculum," claiming it was the world's number one entrepreneur program even before it gained that recognition. I had faith that it would help countless individuals worldwide. The mission of the Millionaire Mastermind Academy is to end poverty through entrepreneurship.

When I shared my vision with Joe Lubick, he expressed his full support. Within a week, I received a $50,000 cashier's check, but that was just the beginning. Joe's investment sparked a national movement. Corporate sponsors came on board, government agencies got involved, and the media took notice. What started as a single moment of faith evolved into a multi-million-dollar infrastructure for change.

The women who participated in the program launched successful businesses, with many achieving six-figure revenues. Some have even become household names and partnered with major retail chains like Walmart and Target to get their products on store shelves.

Importantly, Joe didn't invest in me because we resembled each other. In fact, we come from very different backgrounds; he's Jewish, and I'm a proud Black woman. However, we shared a greater bond: a desire to make a positive impact on the world. We both believe that true impact extends beyond merely accumulating wealth. There's a biblical saying that the wealth of the wicked is being stored for the righteous.

Our focus was on intention. When intention aligns with purpose and faith, anything is possible. This is where stewardship comes in. Many people possess unimaginable wealth yet lack a sense of purpose. The world is filled with those who climb the ladder of success, only to discover they leaned it against the wrong wall. Wealth without wisdom is merely noise, wealth without impact is waste, and wealth without obedience is simply accumulation.

I challenge the wealthy, the high-net-worth individuals, and the ultra-successful to reflect: what seeds are you sowing? You reap in purpose what you sow in faith. The principle of sowing and reaping transcends the Bible; it is a universal law.

As Galatians 6:7 states, *"Do not be deceived: God cannot be mocked. A man reaps what he sows."* Let's explore the true meaning of this principle.

You can't reap a harvest from seeds you didn't plant. You cannot find purpose by hoarding resources, nor can you change lives by simply sitting on your gifts. Every action is a seed; every decision, donation, relationship, and affirmation is part of what determines your harvest.

I've experienced both sides of this equation: I've been the one sowing from nothing, believing for a breakthrough, and I've also reaped the rewards of faithfulness, standing on stages, speaking to thousands, receiving multi-million dollar contracts, advising federal government agencies, and witnessing lives change because of one act of obedience.

I can tell you that the harvest doesn't come easy, but it does come. I remember landing in Arizona, and it was all by faith.

In Atlanta, I met my dear friend Cameron Robb. At that time, she was the senior business development person for the Greater Phoenix Economic Council. She shared valuable information about Phoenix, Arizona, and explained how the work I was doing would greatly benefit the area. I felt privileged that she had recruited my consulting company and the initiatives of the Millionaire Mastermind Academy to spark change in Arizona.

At that moment, I didn't fully realize why I was being called to the desert. Yes, the desert, a place where the heat can be unbearable, reaching up to 120 degrees in the summer! I often joke that if you want to know if you're going to hell, just visit Phoenix in the summertime; it's like a pit stop before hell. The audience always laughs, but honestly, summer in Phoenix can feel that extreme!

Five years later, Cameron Robb is still a phenomenal friend. We connected instantly, and she recognized something in me. She believed that Arizona needed my leadership. Soon, I found myself before the City of Scottsdale's Economic Development Department, presenting to executives from Arizona State University and key decision makers eager to diversify the economy and support small businesses and underserved entrepreneurs.

I had a blueprint and faith. Because I had already been sowing seeds in my previous work with thousands of entrepreneurs, I was ready for this new opportunity. God opened the doors for me.

I had faith, and I had the blueprint. My impact had made headlines; various news outlets and media were talking about the significant work I had accomplished. When I was recruited to Arizona, the community was ready for change. At that time, the mayor of Scottsdale had just passed an anti-discrimination ordinance and said, "We need her here."

I was offered office space at Arizona State University and became the first Black woman to have an office on ASU's Scottsdale campus. I formed partnerships with economic development agencies, large utility companies, and major financial institutions to put resources in the hands of entrepreneurs in Arizona, aimed at changing the data and improving outcomes for the community.

My mission for the nonprofit is to end poverty through entrepreneurship, and my purpose in life aligns with that mission. I believe that poverty is a state of mind.

For a long time, I have been sowing in secret. It's what you do in secret that yields public rewards. People see my success, but they don't know my struggles.

I have been leading prayer calls every Friday morning for years, building people up and speaking life into them. Even during times when I didn't feel uplifted myself, I continued to sow seeds of hope and faith.

Fast forward through my journey: one of my programs was recognized as the state's largest by Governor Katie Hobbs in 2023. This program, celebrated for its impact through public-private partnerships, has helped entrepreneurs secure millions of dollars in contracting opportunities. We've helped them build infrastructure and develop successful companies.

As a result, we began to change the data in Arizona. I partnered with a dear friend, Robin Reed, who sadly passed away in February 2024. Robin was the former president and CEO of the Black Chamber of Arizona and had dedicated eight years to this role.

I had only been in Arizona for three and a half years when I received the news of Robin's passing. It hit me hard, especially because Robin and I had worked closely together. He had been excited about our partnership through my statewide Impact AZ program and the Contracting Readiness Program, and he'd believed this collaboration would significantly impact the state's economy by helping small businesses gain the access they desperately needed.

When I learned about Robin's death after his stroke, my heart sank. I found myself asking, "Why now, Lord? We are just starting." I fell into mourning, struggling to understand the loss.

Robin and I often discussed the idea of him passing the baton to me, as he'd expressed his belief that I would be an excellent leader. At the time, however, I wasn't even considering taking on a role with the statewide chamber; I was still focused on my consulting company.

Currently, I run multiple companies and serve on twenty-one boards. I mentor entrepreneurs across the country and provide advice to both public and private organizations. I guide communities and municipalities in engaging their constituents and creating positive change.

A few days after I learned of Robin's passing, Marshall Franklin, a respected leader in Arizona, asked whether I would step into the role of president and CEO of the Arizona Black Chamber. I now oversee that chamber, focusing on economic impact programs that help thousands of minority-owned businesses access the training, funding, and mentorship needed for growth.

This is what faith looks like.

Let me share a powerful story from the book of Daniel. Shadrach, Meshach, and Abednego were thrown into a fiery furnace for refusing to bow to false gods. They didn't know what the outcome would be; there was no safety net. They followed their convictions, not convenience.

As they stood in that fire, the king looked in and saw a fourth figure, the presence of God Himself walking with them. When they emerged from the flames, the Bible says they didn't even smell like smoke.

Let me tell you, faith will prevent you from carrying the scent of your struggles. Faith will protect your destiny, even when the fire gets hot. But you must be willing to stand in the fire.

This is an essential lesson for wealthy individuals and everyone else to understand: you will be tested. Your generosity will be tested. Your commitment to the greater good will be tested. However, those who sow in faith, like myself, Joe Lubeck, Cameron Robb, and Shadrach, Meshach, and Abednego, will reap in purpose. The ripple effect of one meaningful seed can be profound.

Let's return to Joe for a moment. That one $500 seed created a ripple effect. Hundreds of women have received funding through grants and investment capital. Over 8,000 entrepreneurs were served, and more than twenty national partners were engaged within a two-year span, following the $50,000 donation. Programs expanded to support women across the country, including those in shelters, women exiting the prison system, students in inner-city schools, government-led incubators, and high-level professionals. Millions of lives have been touched, and it all started with that one seed.

So I ask you, what would the world look like if more people sowed like Joe? What if the wealthy stopped chasing mere returns on investment (ROI) and instead pursued eternal significance to drive meaningful change? What if we began asking not how much we can give, but how much impact we can create?

What if we moved beyond merely checking boxes? Let's break this down practically. This is a lesson in leadership.

Here's our **harvest map** to guide you. Every leader, wealthy or otherwise, needs a harvest map. Here's how to build one:

1. **Identify Your Seeds:** Seeds can be your talents, time, resources, or relationships.

2. **Sow Them Intentionally:** Invest in good soil. Spend your resources on people and projects that are innovating and positively disrupting the system to create a better economy and future.

3. **Sow Where the Need Is Urgent:** Research to find who is genuinely making an impact. While many organizations target large institutions, smaller organizations like the Millionaire Mastermind Academy are creating significant change through public-private collaborations. We need the opportunity to invest more seeds into these efforts with your help.

4. **Trust the Process:** Understand that you won't reap the harvest in the same season that you plant, but you will reap in time.

5. **Audit Your Seed Life:** Reflect on what you sowed into last year. Where did you hold back? Where could you have done more? What does your tree of impact look like? The Bible teaches us to judge a tree by the fruit it bears.

Before we conclude, I want you to take out a pen and write down the following questions:

- What are the last three things you gave without expecting anything in return, other than impact?

- What part of your purpose have you buried because you were too busy being successful on your own terms?

- What would your legacy look like if your finances were aligned with impact? If your actions reflected impact and purpose-driven leadership?

This is the power of purpose-driven leadership. You don't exist just to exist; you were created to solve a problem.

If you have the resources to help move our nation forward, that is what true change looks like. You don't just create profit; you create progress. You build people and leave behind a harvest that continues to grow long after you are gone.

Let's lead differently and give intentionally. Let's build legacies that can't be erased, because we sow in faith what we reap in purpose.

I believe my mission of ending poverty through entrepreneurship serves as my navigation system. Everything I do, every opportunity I pursue, revolves around bridging the gap.

If something doesn't align with my overall mission, it doesn't mean it's not worthwhile; it simply may not be right for me. For ultra-successful and wealthy people trying to determine where to invest their resources, the first step is to ensure their efforts align with the change they want to make. They should seek tangible impacts because many people receive significant funding, millions of dollars, without delivering real results.

There are ways to look up testimonials and request impact statements; a little extra due diligence can go a long way. However, wealthy individuals often have limited time, which is why they may choose to invest in established organizations that have been around for decades, even if those organizations aren't making significant impacts.

Conducting research, engaging in conversations, and supporting those who are truly making a difference is essential.

Another important indicator is to monitor conversations. If someone is focused solely on financials and not discussing impact, that should raise a red flag. Personally, I don't discuss money until it's absolutely necessary; I focus on impact first. Only then do I explain why additional resources are needed to continue this important work.

It's crucial to discern where to invest your efforts. This is especially important for people with platforms and significant resources. I often share my **five discernment questions** to help guide this process:

1. **Is the soil fertile?** This means assessing whether the organization or person has a proven track record and a clear mission.

2. **Is the assignment aligned?** Does the effort reflect your values and the calling you believe you have from God?

3. **Is there fruit already evident?** Can you see any impact, even if it's in its early stages?

4. **Is the motive pure?** Are you giving out of a sense of obedience rather than performance or manipulation?

5. **Is this a faith seed?** Does this investment stretch you in a way that requires you to trust God with the outcome?

It's essential to use these questions when deciding where to sow your resources. I find them incredibly valuable.

Let me provide some clear examples of where to invest for practical returns on investment (ROI). One key area is generational change. To achieve this, we need to invest in curriculum development and support organizations like the Millionaire Mastermind Academy, as well as youth leadership organizations and local chambers throughout the country. These investments contribute to economic empowerment and entrepreneurial training programs.

Another important aspect of generational change is ensuring access for underserved groups. This involves investing in coalitions that work to bridge racial wealth gaps, crucial for achieving equitable opportunities.

We also need to focus on women in leadership. This means investing in nonprofits that mentor single mothers, support women founders, and uplift Black women and other underrepresented women of color.

Lastly, to achieve scalable impact, we must invest in ventures that address systemic issues across health, housing, finance, and other pressing challenges. These are all examples of where meaningful investment can lead to significant change.

CHAPTER 8

EXPANSION BY FAITH: FROM ATLANTA TO ARIZONA

I want you to lean in with me right now because there comes a moment when vision becomes larger than your current location. When faith compels you to step into new territory, when God says "go," leaders discover that expansion by faith is not merely about growth; it's about aligning with purpose.

This chapter is intended for senior executives, corporate leaders, nonprofit CEOs, or anyone who feels called to achieve more than what they currently see in their scope.

For me, it all began with a ride.

At the time, I was living in Atlanta, and I had the opportunity to give Cameron Robb a ride. Less than a year later, I found myself expanding to Arizona. But something shifted in that moment. It wasn't just a ride; it was a divine appointment.

During our conversation, we discussed data and underserved markets, and I shared my work on ecosystem building, emphasizing the lack of funding, resources, and support for entrepreneurs. It felt like a calling. Moving from

Houston to Atlanta was one thing, but transitioning from Atlanta to Arizona, stepping into a new state, new climate, and new ecosystem while carrying a purpose that required faith was an entirely different experience.

I became the first Black woman to have an office on the Arizona State University campus. I established relationships and connected with incredible people. We began to see a change in statistics, with minority-owned businesses and underrepresented contractors being awarded contracts. It wasn't just a ride for the sake of it; it was a divine appointment and a pivotal moment in my journey. I was determined to make an impact.

We launched Impact AZ, my nonprofit organization, in partnership with the Black Chamber of Arizona under Robin Reed's leadership. Impact AZ was intentionally designed to intersect with both the corporate and public sectors, with a focus on contracting readiness for small, underserved businesses.

I remember standing before a room filled with Arizona business leaders, government officials, and investors, declaring that we would help entrepreneurs secure contracts. I had successfully executed similar initiatives in other markets and possessed a blueprint to do it again; I just needed someone to believe in me.

Initially, I faced skepticism because I was new to the market, and people were trying to determine how I would accomplish what I was proposing. I would tell them, "I have a program dedicated to helping entrepreneurs gain access to contracts." I understood the small-business landscape because I had been a small-business owner and learned to bootstrap a business.

Our first investor in Phoenix, Arizona, was JPMorgan Chase. They believed in my vision and my passion for entrepreneurship. They granted $200,000 in sponsorship to launch the Impact AZ program, which has since become the largest accelerator program in the state, helping entrepreneurs gain access to contracts.

The funding wasn't used for events and photo opportunities; in fact, it didn't fund those at all. It funded access and essential programs. It provided legal advisory services for entrepreneurs, certification assistance, and matchmaking opportunities between corporations and startups. It also funded readiness training and developed an app. Entrepreneurs in our first cohort secured contracts with local governments, some even with NFL franchises, and partnered with major tech companies.

The difference is that we aren't just teaching business; we are teaching faith-driven innovation, strategic access and impact, and purpose-driven leadership. This is what expansion by faith looks like in leadership: You leverage divine appointments, pivotal moments, and words that can shift your trajectory. You cross boundaries of comfort, both external and internal.

Internal comfort relates to mindset. You collaborate with institutions, corporations, and government entities with the sole purpose of fostering partnerships. You build programs that bridge existing gaps. Purpose-driven leadership in senior positions requires you to see what others do not.

Then you create the infrastructure necessary to advance others.

Now, let's look at some data to understand why this is important. In 2025, Gen Z and millennials made up the majority of the workforce. According to a Deloitte survey conducted that year, 89 percent of millennials and 92 percent of Gen Z respondents reported that a sense of purpose is crucial for job satisfaction. However, many leaders, particularly those from older generations, have not adapted to this shift.

This lack of adaptation has led to turnover and disappointment in the workplace. As leaders, especially senior leaders, we risk becoming irrelevant if we do not embrace the call for purpose-driven leadership, as the next generation demands intentional purpose, impact, and meaning in their work.

If we fail to expand our approach, we may maintain our numbers but lose market share.

Now, let's discuss some outcomes and testimonials. Entrepreneurs who were previously ineligible for public contracts are now bidding on and winning them. Underserved entrepreneurs are securing contracts with school districts, and women from marginalized neighborhoods are seeing their dreams funded. They are receiving mentorship and creating job opportunities while solving pressing problems. Corporate partners have expressed their support, saying, "Dr. Velma, we see you, we believe in you, and we want to work with you."

One woman who previously held a low-wage job secured a contract for a large municipal project after participating in Impact AZ. She assembled a small team and increased her revenue by 300 percent in just one year. Now she mentors other women in our network. These are not just small victories; they are generational ripples.

As we conclude this chapter, I want to introduce the **Expansion Leadership Model**, a framework designed for senior leaders and those who aspire to lead with purpose at scale.

1. **Divine Call:** Recognize a moment of clarity or an invitation that transcends logic.

2. **Strategic Entry:** Determine the best place to establish your efforts. This could be a state, sector, or system. Cultivate partnerships and conduct thorough research.

3. **Resource Alignment:** Ensure alignment of funding, personnel, and infrastructure. Commit value and invest financially to drive progress.

4. **Access Advocacy:** Work to eliminate barriers for others, addressing contract systems, certifications, influence, and technical assistance. Collaborate with entrepreneurs rather than compete with them. Too many corporations are hiring employees to fill entrepreneurial roles that should be held by business owners working together to advance shared goals.

   Here's something I want to share with you: Entrepreneurs tend to gather with other entrepreneurs, while corporate professionals often associate with other corporate people.

   How can we expect a corporate professional to provide entrepreneurial advice? This disconnect is one reason we're not seeing progress in data movement. Corporations and government entities need to collaborate with business owners like myself, programs such as the Millionaire Mastermind Academy, and innovative leaders and entrepreneurs across the country who have built and sold companies.

5. **Measure and Multiply:** It's essential to track outcomes, celebrate successes, and let your results attract more opportunities.

Reflection Questions:

- What territory is God urging you to explore?

- What discomfort must you embrace to achieve growth?

- Who are the partners, corporations, or public institutions that can help you scale your impact?

- What metrics will you track to ensure you're not just checking boxes but actually making an impact?

Expansion by faith isn't merely about ticking off tasks; it's about your influence, integrity, and alignment.

If you feel afraid, that's completely okay. Let your faith guide you anyway.

Today, I declare that you will be bold. You will take action. You are a winner. You are above, not beneath. You are a purpose-driven leader, a trailblazer, and an innovator. You are a solution to a problem, and you will expand for a greater purpose, an eternal purpose.

CHAPTER 9

FIGHTING EVIL GATEKEEPERS: A BATTLE FOR EQUITY

Leadership isn't just about having a vision and expanding opportunities; it's also about creating access for those who are underserved.

Often, access is guarded by what I refer to as "evil gatekeepers" and sometimes by spiritual forces of darkness. This chapter is for you, the reader; it is for purpose-driven leaders who recognize the gap between potential and the obstacles posed by these gatekeepers.

It's for those who have been blocked by people who hold the keys to resources.

Let's take a moment to define what an evil gatekeeper is. In a neutral sense, an evil gatekeeper is someone who controls access to resources, networks, capital, and influence. However, evil gatekeepers hoard access to power and opportunities out of fear, prejudice, or a desire to maintain control.

Evil gatekeepers spread lies and slander to protect their harmful agendas. They use systems to block people, especially people of color or those with purpose, from stepping into important roles. They create barriers in hiring, funding, and contracts, intentionally or through neglect.

The actions of these gatekeepers are often hidden. They may present themselves as advisors, mentors, critics, or even friends, saying things like, "You're too experienced," "You're too radical," or "Your message is too strong." They keep you waiting on the promise of opportunities without any real progress.

To understand the gravity of this situation, we can refer to Ephesians 6:12: *"For we do not wrestle against flesh and blood, but against principalities, powers, rulers of darkness, and spiritual hosts of wickedness in heavenly places."* Many people try to fight spiritual battles in the physical realm, but you cannot win a spiritual battle by merely addressing the physical aspects.

Instead, you must engage in spiritual warfare through prayer, fasting, and deepening your relationship with God. Many attempt to fight these battles by targeting those around them or by striving to change outcomes directly, which can lead to feelings of defeat and exhaustion.

You will lose every time if you only combat evil gatekeepers in the physical realm without exercising your spiritual authority. We need to fight spiritually through discernment, prayer, fasting, and a commitment to truth. Ultimately, it is the truth that will set a nation free.

I want to share some personal experiences with evil gatekeepers. When I first became the president and CEO of the Black Chamber of Arizona, lies and rumors were spread about me. People conspired to silence my voice and reduce my impact. This created a climate of fear among those seeking to access resources, hindering progress due to the deceitful narratives being circulated.

Despite these challenges, I remained steadfast. I continued to pray, do the right thing for others, show up with a smile, and engage positively. Gradually, things began to shift. When I stood firm, prayed with my leadership team, sought clarity, and spoke the truth with humility, I not only survived the slander but also opened doors of opportunity.

Many corporate partners, not only in Arizona but throughout the country, began to see me as a leader changing the narrative on access in America. It was not an easy journey; I had to fight and stand firm in my faith.

I had to pray. I needed to ask God for strength and to cover me.

I sought divine insight, wisdom, and knowledge. I prayed for destiny helpers. What are destiny helpers? Well, Jesus had twelve disciples, and he knew that one of them would betray him. Similarly, I prayed for the right people to support me in my mission.

Even though it was difficult to ignore some of the negative things people were saying about me, I realized that the true battle is in our minds. The Bible tells us that the devil's job is to steal, kill, and destroy.

This is evident in our country today, where suicide rates are at an all-time high and mental health issues are rampant. We face killings, wars, assassination attempts, and even successful assassinations. All of this aligns with the devil's mission to kill, steal, and destroy.

Spiritual warfare is a confrontation between the Kingdom of Heaven and the kingdom of darkness. We are caught between these two spiritual forces, which are vying for us. The Kingdom of Heaven embodies light, positivity, and progress, aligned with all the fruits of the Spirit. The kingdom of darkness represents the opposite.

God promises us life and abundance. Jeremiah 29:11 states, *"'For I know the plans I have for you,' declares the Lord, 'plans to prosper you, not to harm you, and plans to give you hope and a future.'"* Many of us are not experiencing the promises God has declared over us because we are often unaware of our actions. We allow heavy burdens, false burdens, and negative influences to sabotage us and divert us from our paths.

Therefore, we need to pray for discernment and understand the difference between spiritual battles and physical frustrations. We must recognize that we are fighting against evil gatekeepers, principalities, powers, and rulers of darkness, as well as spiritual hosts of wickedness on earth.

Here are some **leadership strategies for senior-level professionals** to combat gatekeepers and avoid becoming one themselves:

1. **Discernment:** Train your spiritual senses to identify when pushback is oppression and when it's simply part of growth.

2. **Strategic Prayer and Fasting**: Prepare spiritually before launching new initiatives.

3. **Networking with Purpose:** Build alliances across race, sectors, and generations.

4. **Transparent Communication:** Slander thrives in darkness. Don't allow gossip to fester within your organization. Remove those with a gossiping mentality, as their approach reflects how they handle everything.

5. **Resilient Identity:** Know who you are and your purpose. Understand the vision you are fighting for. As a purpose-driven leader, you won't be troubled by slander. Life is only 10 percent what happens to us and 90 percent how we respond. Being confident in your identity prevents slander from undermining you.

This is why this book is so vital at this time.

Considering the data and context, the issue of purpose generation versus gatekeeper blockage is significant. According to Deloitte, 89.92 percent of millennials and Gen Z believe that a sense of purpose is essential at work. When gatekeepers refuse to adapt or relinquish control, young leaders often leave, resulting in high turnover in rigid cultures. Surveys indicate that many younger professionals feel stifled by structures that do not prioritize purpose, innovation, or moral alignment. This conflict is impersonal, generational, systemic, and spiritual.

I remember when a group of doubters said that I could not bring about the change I wanted to see. They claimed I was aiming too high and challenged everything I was doing.

Well, they certainly tried to challenge my efforts. However, every morning, I woke up ready to battle. I prayed for clarity, strength, wisdom, godly knowledge, zeal, and the spiritual backbone of steel to stand firm against adversity, evil spirits, and the gatekeepers who sought to keep God's people in bondage. I prayed for these evil gatekeepers to be exposed, not out of anger but in truth. And one by one, that happened.

Evil gatekeepers feel threatened by your mission and purpose, which God has placed within you. They are insecure and resort to lies, slander, and sowing discord. They do not want to see change because of their self-serving agendas.

To this day, I still fight against evil gatekeepers. I thank God for the gift of discernment, which keeps my spirit alert to their presence. I can see them from afar.

Here's a model for leaders to use to overcome gatekeepers:

1. **Expose:** Identify who or what is blocking progress.

2. **Engage:** We must approach this challenge with collaboration and, when necessary, confrontation, always rooted in truth. We cannot be afraid to confront the obstacles preventing us from moving forward.

3. **Empower:** We need to support allies and elevate those making an impact whose efforts are being obstructed by evil gatekeepers.

4. **Establish:** Build new systems that do not rely on old gatekeepers. We must create equitable pathways for all.

Reflection Questions:

- Who are the gatekeepers in your ecosystem that are preventing your organization or community from advancing?

- In what areas are you fighting spiritually but attempting to win physically?

- What truth do you need to speak to release evil gatekeepers from your ecosystems and their harmful assignments?

- How will you lead differently, understanding the concept of evil gatekeepers, not only for yourself but also for those being held back?

To everyone reading this, the battle for access is real, but you are not powerless. You have been given the authority to tread on serpents and scorpions. If you are a purpose-driven leader designed for seasons like these, if you are a leader disrupting systems and creating change from within organizations, I declare that you will walk in clarity. I declare you will lead even when it comes with sorrow or risk.

I decree and declare that you will walk boldly into your purpose and destiny, even if it means facing the possibility of being fired from your job. You may lose a job, but you can never lose your purpose. When one door closes, if you are walking in alignment, another door is already open.

I decree and declare that you will break through. I decree and declare that your works will be seen and will make an impact. I decree and declare that you will expand your influence and your voice and actions will solve problems. I decree and declare that you will leave the gates open for the generations that come after you.

CHAPTER 10

PURPOSE OVER POLITICS: REDEFINING LEADERSHIP

What does it mean to redefine leadership? It requires a shift from traditional models to more empathetic, inclusive approaches that can navigate a world marked by rapid technological change and evolving expectations.

I often say we must innovate at the speed of relevance. You are not here to be mediocre; you are here to lead in this crucial moment in history. Today, when politics often divides rather than unites, when access is primarily reserved for the wealthy and influential, and when voices become quieter as resources tighten, a call is emerging from leaders like you.

This is about purpose over politics. Politics will always change, parties will evolve, and laws will rise and fall. However, the purpose, the reason you were put on this earth to solve a particular issue, remains unchanged. That purpose may lie dormant now, but it is still within you.

This chapter aims to awaken the giant inside you and emphasizes the importance of redefining leadership. It reorients leadership from fleeting influence to lasting legacy, focusing on systems that outlive individual personalities.

It's about building resilience in the face of cultural storms and discarding practices that do not serve our communities or our purpose.

Let's discuss the Arizona paradox. I moved to Arizona due to what I believe was a divine appointment, only to discover a paradox: a state abundant in opportunity, innovation, and tech funding yet plagued by significant gaps in racial and economic equality. Universities here produce remarkable innovations, but many communities are excluded from contracts. While wealth flows in, it does not reach under-resourced neighborhoods adequately.

Data supports what I have observed. Numerous corporations are investing millions in tech and infrastructure, yet minority-owned businesses account for only a small share of those contracts. There are disparities in entrepreneurial support; underserved entrepreneurs lack access to capital, mentorship, and essential opportunities.

This issue is not confined to Arizona; it is a global concern and occurs across America. When I launched Impact AZ, a contracting readiness program designed to help underserved entrepreneurs build sustainable, successful companies that can endure any political or economic climate, my vision extended beyond the program itself. I sought to create a system of equitable access that outlasts any single leader.

Through contracting readiness, I teach entrepreneurs how to qualify for, bid on, and manage contracts and to form strategic partnerships across the public, private, and civic sectors. This approach avoids tokenism and emphasizes measurable outcomes, providing infrastructure for continuous mentorship, business certification, and compliance maintenance.

By building such systems, we change the narrative from who gets in to how anyone can succeed with the right tools.

This has been my primary focus for over a decade. In 2022, I was honored with a Presidential Lifetime Achievement Award by the White House for helping thousands of entrepreneurs escape the cycle of poverty.

I have developed programs and curricula for economic development agencies, cities, corporations, and financial institutions. I am proud to report that we've witnessed a transformation in the data. We have seen history change before our eyes.

Minority entrepreneurs are gaining access to contracts. Small businesses that once operated as one-person shows are now firms that employ many people, contributing to the GDP and the economy. There is power in the purchasing power of the Black community and underrepresented markets.

If corporations wish to sustain themselves, they must create solutions to existing problems and support small businesses in their growth.

They must help to move the needle forward because our economy is primarily composed of small businesses. I will say it again: when you build equitable systems, you shift the narrative from who gets in to how many people we can uplift.

Yes, I've received recognition all over the country, including various awards. Impact AZ was declared the state's largest entrepreneurial program by Governor Hobbs, the current governor of Arizona. However, recognition is a byproduct and not the goal. I always say that seeking dominion is not the pursuit; it is the result.

The aim is to change lives: small business owners landing contracts, new companies employing people in underserved neighborhoods, and generational wealth beginning to take root. One of my favorite scriptures states that the wealth of the wicked is being stored up for the righteous.

In fact, let me share this scripture. Proverbs 13:22 reads, *"A good man leaves an inheritance to his children's children, and the wealth of the wicked is laid up for the righteous."* In another translation, it says, *"A good man leaves an inheritance to his grandchildren, but the wealth of a sinner is stored up for the righteous."* Yet another reads, *"If you obey God, you will have something to leave your grandchildren. If you don't obey God, those who live right will get what you leave."*

There are many translations, but the message is clear: If we are to leave an inheritance for our children's children, it is crucial that we recognize that purpose takes precedence over politics. We must integrate purpose into our actions. Too often, leadership books pit personality against systems as if they were mutually exclusive.

However, I have discovered that strong, purpose-driven personalities are the bridge that builds robust systems. Personality acts as the catalyst, the voice, boldness, and courage, while systems provide structure, reliability, longevity, and sustainability. Without purpose-driven leaders, systems can become stagnant. Conversely, without systems, personalities may fizzle out when opposition arises.

You, with your voice, zeal, purpose, fire, and faith, are meant to train others to become agents of change. This includes mentoring, holding space for others, and building frameworks that can support thousands, even when you are no longer able to manage every detail. We need purpose-driven leadership, especially in this climate that resists diversity, equity, and inclusion (DEI) initiatives.

Currently, DEI programs are under attack. Many companies have rolled back diversity policies amid backlash. But the truth is this: diversity results from doing the right thing; it is a business imperative. Studies show that companies that double down on inclusion outperform those that retreat.

Consumers, employees, and shareholders increasingly expect authenticity. They view DEI not as politics but as a matter of moral clarity and opportunity. Purpose-driven leadership means leaning into these challenges and building stronger infrastructures for inclusive leadership.

According to Census Bureau projections, the U.S. will become majority minority by 2045. Additionally, in the past ten years, 40 percent of Fortune 500 companies have been displaced or disrupted by purpose-driven entrepreneurs. We must develop infrastructure to support the next generation of leaders. Inclusive programs must be integrated into business strategy, not as an afterthought but as a core value and competitive differentiator.

I would like to share some tools and frameworks for leaders to guide their actions beyond politics. I refer to this as **my framework for building legacy systems**.

1. **Vision Clarity:** What is your non-negotiable purpose?

2. **Stakeholder Mapping:** Who needs to be at the table? Consider the communities and private sector representatives that should be included.

3. **Barrier Identification:** What political or systemic gatekeepers are blocking access? Identify the policies or implicit biases that exist in awarding contracts, hiring from underserved communities, and within your procurement department.

4. **System Design:** Create pipelines, processes, mentorship opportunities, accountability measures, compliance frameworks, and funding for those who have historically been excluded.

5. **Measurement and Feedback:** We must establish metrics for equity and impact. Use data to adjust and enhance programs.

I had a meeting last year with business developers and civic leaders in Atlanta, where a Black female entrepreneur shared her experience. She had turned down contracts because she did not meet certain certification prerequisites held by large firms. These certifications are expensive and time-consuming, and she felt she lacked the infrastructure to succeed.

Through our program, we helped entrepreneurs secure contracts. She received guidance, mentorship, and capital. As a result, she now has contracts with the NFL and employs over 75 people. This is a perfect example of how providing resources and access to minority and diverse entrepreneurs enables them to demonstrate their value and contribute to the GDP.

Another example involves corporate partners I have worked with who previously did not include minority vendors in their procurement pipeline. They were invited to collaborate on vendor lists, joint mentorship, and shared risk partnerships with new entrepreneurs. These companies reported improvements in brand equity, innovation, and customer loyalty, and increased their bottom line.

Reflection Exercise

Write down one system in your organization or planned domain that feels politically exclusive or inaccessible. Design a plan to open it up. Consider who you will include, what resources they will need, and what policies or practices must change. Identify one committed partner from the private or public sector who can assist you in building that system.

Embrace the principle of "purpose over politics" and demonstrate courage in the face of controversy. It takes faith to act decisively when others play it safe. I reflect on companies that quickly dismantled their diversity, equity, and inclusion (DE&I) initiatives, and I wonder where they will stand when minority groups become the majority in 2025.

It requires faith to build when others are tearing things down. Sustainable leadership is rooted in purpose-driven action. While maintaining our passion and voice, we must remember that purpose-driven leadership is essential, especially in times like these.

A good example of leadership by personality is Donald Trump.

And let me just say this. I am not a Democrat or a Republican. I am an independent thinker.

Trump relies on his image and communication style, often using scare tactics. When I think about our current government, especially the White House and its social media presence, it seems to be predominantly focused on his personality.

During his campaign, he made bold statements and effectively dominated the media, leveraging his unique personality. At present, his personality has become central to the system.

However, this reliance on personality also reveals weaknesses and challenges. Our government currently depends on this media-driven narrative, which is inconsistent and can polarize opinions. When he is absent or loses credibility, as we are witnessing with various international issues, the gaps become more apparent.

When discussing leadership in systems terms, it's important to note that a systems-based approach relies on structures, processes, and institutional frameworks to guide decision-making, accountability, and outcomes, regardless of who the leader is. Many current issues arise because appropriate systems were not established.

For example, a systems-based leader would prioritize clear succession planning, standardized procedures, and equitable policies, rather than allowing policies to fluctuate with a leader's personal preferences. They would implement structured rules that outlast individual personalities.

Equitable systems are essential because they ensure that fairness and justice are integrated into the foundational structure. This is evident in various circumstances, such as the tragic situation involving Charlie Kirk. It was devastating to witness someone shot and killed in broad daylight in front of students.

Similarly, the incident involving George Floyd, where a police officer knelt on his neck for an extended period, was horrendous. It's troubling that people cannot openly discuss Charlie Kirk or express differing opinions without fear, despite his own outspoken nature. People associated with shows like Jimmy Kimmel's are facing firings, and networks are canceling programs indefinitely, all in the name of freedom of speech. Yet, these same voices freely discuss racial injustices related to George Floyd and other heinous crimes.

When I consider equitable systems, it's clear that they are vital for ensuring fairness and justice within our infrastructure, rather than leaving it to a leader's personal preferences. Without equitable systems, personality-driven leadership only amplifies existing inequalities, as favoritism, loyalty, or identity dictates who benefits.

Policies that are shaped solely by personal preferences or biases can harm marginalized communities and lead to unstable outcomes. In contrast, having equitable systems with established rules, processes, accountability, and measures ensures that everyone has access to opportunities, resources, and fair treatment, regardless of who is in charge. This approach is rooted in equity and helps protect against the abuse of power.

Additionally, it reduces dependency on a single leader and fosters trust among diverse groups.

CHAPTER 11

THE POVERTY MINDSET MUST DIE

Poverty is a state of mind. You are not inherently poor; you have simply been programmed to think small. There are mindsets that can keep you poor long after money has arrived. This is why we often see people win the lottery and, just six months later, find themselves broke.

You can make millions and still possess a poverty mindset. Mindset is crucial. You may have a good job, drive a luxury car, hold a C-suite position, or speak at conferences, yet still operate with a poverty mentality.

The poverty mindset is not just about money; it encompasses your sense of purpose and how you perceive yourself. This chapter focuses on the thought patterns and spiritual beliefs that shape your identity: Who do you say you are?

If you don't change what's in your heart, your external world may never change. The same struggles will accompany you from one level to another, from one state to another, and from one job to another. They will follow you wherever you go.

Excellence, purpose, impact, generational wealth, and community transformation are standards you must adopt, not merely goals to be achieved. It is essential to understand that poverty is a state of mind. It is shaped by your thoughts, the words you speak, the people you surround yourself with, and the barriers you impose on yourself.

I want to remind you that I grew up very poor. I was born and raised in an environment where poverty was normalized, pain was inherited, and small thinking was a means of survival. However, I was determined that my future would not mirror my past. Although I had no control over my upbringing, I realized I could change the trajectory of my life.

I began praying and asking God to help me unlearn the negative habits and thought patterns I had about life, people, and wealth. I understood that we must first cultivate wealth in our minds before it can manifest in the physical realm. Remember, life and death are in the power of the tongue.

I have witnessed many brilliant people sabotage their blessings because they didn't believe they deserved more. I have seen entire communities embrace the notion that *this is just the way it is.*

Here's the distinction between a poverty mindset and an abundance mindset: A poverty mindset says, *I can't afford that, I don't have the right connections,* or *People like me don't do things like that.*

A poor mindset is an evil gatekeeper.

A poverty mindset stops you from sowing the seeds that will produce a harvest. An abundance mindset says, *I invest before I see the return. My network is always growing.*

I am a purpose-driven, valuable individual in my community and in the world. I am solving problems the world needs solved.

The abundance mindset says, *If God put the dream in me, He will open the doors. If God gave me the vision, He will provide the resources.*

The abundance mindset states, *When I help others, my life will transform into a lifestyle of greatness and abundance.* It emphasizes building with a legacy in mind.

Abundant thinkers don't ask "if"; they ask "how." I remember the moment I realized something had to change. I had built and sold businesses, but something still felt off.

I had reached a level of outward success, yet I was making decisions from a poverty mindset. I often expected rejection before anticipating favor. I would undercharge, overwork, and shrink in rooms where I was meant to solve problems.

Some of you may be wondering why, and some of you may be facing the same situation right now. The answer is that I was still carrying the spirit of poverty. I had not renewed my mind.

Let me reference a scripture that resonated with me, Romans 12:2, one of my favorites. It reads: *"Do not conform to the pattern of this world, but be transformed by the renewing of your mind. Then you will be able to test and approve what God's will is, His good, pleasing, and perfect will."* I was still carrying the spirit of poverty because I had not renewed my mind.

You must renew your thinking. You have to be transformed by the renewing of your mind. Only then will you be able to test and approve what God's will is.

I had to let go of my old mindset. I had to grieve for it and bury it.

I needed to let go of how I was raised, what people said I could or couldn't do, and how culture taught me to play small. Only after that could I begin to see true overflow in my impact, income, and influence.

This brings me back to when I launched the Millionaire Mastermind Academy, a nonprofit focused on ending poverty through entrepreneurship. When I started it, I knew I wanted to help women. I recognized I had solutions to significant problems, but I didn't know how to end poverty through entrepreneurship. This effort is still ongoing; we are writing history right now.

I could have thought, *No one will invest in me. No one will see this as a solution.* However, I chose to keep pouring in, sowing seeds, leading with purpose, and speaking those things as though they already were. I continued to solve problems. In doing so, I not only changed my own mindset but also helped millions of others change theirs.

One woman entered the Millionaire Mastermind Academy with a powerful idea but was broken in belief. She thought no one would take her seriously and believed that living in the projects was her destiny.

We began with mindset training before delving into business strategy. I told her, "Your bank account does not define your net worth. Your idea is valuable, but you must first believe in it. You need to walk in faith, not by sight."

Faith is the substance of things hoped for and the evidence of things not seen. She started showing up differently and began asking questions.

She invested her time and attended every class without fail. A year and a half later, she pitched her idea at a funding summit.

She received her first grant. Fast forward to today: she owns a well-known, growing wellness business that employs people and gives back to her community. The money didn't change her; her mindset did.

I'd like to share another story.

A corporate executive attended one of my training sessions. He had been stuck in middle management for over a decade. He was brilliant, kind, and quiet. He confided in me, saying, "I just don't think I'm leadership material."

I asked him, "Who told you that? Why did you believe it? And why did you believe them?"

That moment unlocked something in him. He began leading economic development work internally, created a mentorship circle for young Black men, and became a sought-after speaker, earning hundreds of thousands of dollars to date.

He didn't need a promotion; he just needed permission to think abundantly.

Now, because I focus on data, I want to share what the statistics say. According to Gallup, 42 percent of employee turnover is preventable, primarily due to misalignment of purpose rather than pay.

Millions are quitting high-paying jobs despite economic uncertainty. Why? Because people desire purpose, not just paychecks. This information comes from the Bureau of Labor Statistics.

In an anti-DEI climate, many companies are retreating. However, according to Sustainable Brands and PRovoke Media, those who remain committed to purpose are outperforming their competitors.

We must pay attention to this data.

I want to teach you **how to overcome a poverty mindset** because it cannot simply be educated away; it must be spiritually uprooted and practically retrained. Here's how:

1. **Truth Replacement:** We need to identify the lies that have been spoken over our lives and speak the truth louder. For example, the lie

that says you will never be wealthy or amount to anything is false. The truth is that you have the mind of Christ and access to heavenly ideas, as the Bible tells us we are created in the image of Jesus Christ. Another lie might be that you're too old or that it's too late. The truth is that you were born for such a time as this.

2. **Value and Excellence:** Stop asking for discounts on your destiny. If you want to charge premium prices and are solving a problem, your thinking must be premium as well. If you're building a company, do it with excellence, not just for one group or another but for impact. Let your excellence speak for itself.

3. **Faith First:** You have everything within you to take the first step. Don't wait; start now. Look at Noah in the Bible: he built the ark before seeing a single cloud. I have built several of my companies with no investors, created curricula before I had contracts, and invested in others before receiving donations. Move in faith. Noah built the ark first, and then the rain came later.

4. **Think Community and Mentorship:** Proximity is power. You cannot break free from poverty alone. Surround yourself with those who support and uplift you.

By implementing these strategies, you can begin to shift your mindset towards abundance and success.

You can't break free from a poverty mindset if you are surrounded by small thinkers. Seek out environments where abundance is the norm, where discussing legacy and wealth building is common, and where million-dollar ideas are casually exchanged. Embrace a standard of excellence.

Stop labeling yourself as a small Black business or a minority business owner and using that as an excuse for mediocrity. Being Black, brown, female, disabled, or underrepresented should not lower your standards.

Excellence is your superpower. When JPMorgan Chase invested in my entrepreneurial program, Impact AZ, it wasn't just because of my inspiring story. It was because our data, systems, delivery, curriculum, and execution were all excellent.

Excellence opens doors that your background may not. I want to share four scriptures and spiritual anchors:

1. Proverbs 23:7: *"As a man thinketh in his heart, so is he."* Your thoughts shape your habits.

2. Romans 12:2: *"Be transformed by the renewing of your mind."* Your life cannot change until your mind does.

3. Hebrews 11:1: *"Now faith is the substance of things hoped for."* If you can already see it, that's not faith.

4. Proverbs 18:16: *"A man's gift maketh room for him and bringeth him before great men."* The New Living Translation puts it this way: *"Giving a gift can open doors; it gives access to important people."*

I went from giving everything to others, burning myself out, and being afraid to charge what I was worth or to claim my purpose to finally believing that wealth and impact can coexist with purpose and peace. Once I accepted this, I began developing scalable curricula. I started receiving calls from government agencies and Fortune 500 companies.

I was invited into rooms I never sought out. I built and sold companies and helped thousands of entrepreneurs rise above poverty. None of this would have been possible if I had remained mentally poor or broken.

I want to help you reset your mind. Here's an exercise:

Step 1: Identify the Lies

Write down three limiting beliefs you've held about yourself or your work. Examples: *"People like me don't succeed," "No one wants to do business with me," "No one in my family is wealthy," "I'm too young,"* or *"I'm too old to start over."*

Step 2: Write Truths to Replace Them

For each lie, write a counter-truth rooted in scripture, legacy, or logic.

Step 3: Act in Opposition to the Lie

Over the next thirty days, do one bold thing that contradicts the lie. Apply for the grant, pitch your program, raise your prices, hire a coach, sow the seed, start your business, move to a new city, or end relationships that don't value you. Embrace your "go" moment.

Here's a closing declaration. Say this out loud wherever you are:

> *"I release everything the enemy used to keep me in bondage. I release every thought that tells me I'm not enough. I rebuke small thinking and false humility. I was created to create. I was created to solve problems. I am not bound by what I see. I walk by faith. I plant in faith, and I reap in purpose. The poverty mindset dies with me, and my children will inherit abundance. I am not poor; I am powerful."*

Now, think like it, walk like it, and build like it because the poverty mindset must die so that your purpose can live.

Excellence builds trust, and in the realms of business and leadership, trust is a form of currency. Clients, partners, employees, and investors all gauge credibility through consistency.

Delivering excellence means that people know they can rely on you. For instance, when you think of brands like Mercedes-Benz or Chick-fil-A, you immediately associate them with a commitment to excellence. In contrast, mediocrity erodes trust, while excellence reinforces it.

In a crowded marketplace, excellence differentiates you from the competition. Customers may not remember average service, but they will remember experiences characterized by precision, care, and quality. Leaders who embody excellence set a standard within their organizations, fostering a culture where exceptional performance becomes the norm.

Moreover, excellence attracts opportunities. Those who consistently deliver at a high level become magnets for new chances. Excellence also signifies stewardship; as leaders, we are entrusted with people, resources, and vision. Practicing excellence means making the most of what we have been given and demonstrating respect for the mission of our organization and for those we lead.

For me, excellence is non-negotiable. It is the foundation of credibility, competitiveness, opportunity, stewardship, culture, and character. Without excellence, leadership falters, and businesses lose their edge. When excellence is present, it creates organizations that are trusted, resilient, and built to last.

CHAPTER 12

YOU CAN'T BE FIRED FROM YOUR PURPOSE

I need you to understand this: wherever you are and whoever you are, your job is temporary, but your purpose is eternal. Your job title may end, your corporate contract may be canceled, and doors may close. However, what lives inside you (the call, the vision, the purpose), nothing or no one can take that away from you.

This chapter is for those who have been displaced, laid off, or passed over, as well as for the powerful individuals who have built, led, and scaled yet still feel scared. Purpose bears fruit when everything else fails.

Let's take a moment to consider the current economic and political climate. In 2025, job insecurity is a real issue, and we can no longer pretend otherwise. More than 144,900 people in the tech sector alone have been laid off so far this year. Nearly 86,000 job cuts were announced in August, an alarming 39 percent increase from July. Millions of American workers enter each month already anxious, wondering, *What if this is my last day?* A recent bank rate survey revealed that nearly half of U.S. workers plan to search for new jobs, not because they want to leave, but because they do not feel secure.

These statistics represent real stories, people losing stability and questioning what comes next. But I want you to remember: uncertainty is not your identity. Yes, federal layoffs count in the hundreds of thousands. It may sound chaotic and feel like betrayal, but this is your moment to stop uncertain thinking.

You may not have your current title tomorrow. You may not know your income next month, but you do know what lives within you. Here's how to shift your perspective:

1. Shift your mindset from *What if I lose?* to *How was I made to serve beyond my job?*

2. Shift your strategy from seeking status quo safety to embracing stewardship with courage.

3. Shift your identity from being an employee to becoming an empowered assignment carrier.

Remember, uncertainty doesn't have to hold you back. Purpose can set you free. Here's how to transition from being fired from your job to walking in purpose:

Step 1: Discover the problem you were put on earth to solve. Write down the pain points you or your community have experienced. Identify the problem that keeps you awake at night; that is your clue. Use your gifts, experiences, and story to outline a solution.

Many people ask, "How do I discover my purpose?" Your purpose is the very thing that you were created to do on earth. Reflect on the challenges that should have overwhelmed you, yet you survived and conquered them. That struggle is your purpose; it's what you will help others overcome.

Step 2: Activate your transferable skills. Even if you lose one role, you still possess valuable skills such as leadership, communication, relationship-building, strategy, and consulting. Identify how these skills can translate into new areas, such as speaking engagements, consulting, coaching, digital content creation, or nonprofit leadership.

Step 3: Build your purpose platform. Your platform encompasses your message, medium, and mission. Whether it's a podcast, a book, a small group, or a nonprofit, start planting seeds now. Your platform will signal to the world your passion and purpose.

By following these steps, you can navigate uncertainty and step boldly into your purpose.

The world notices a consistent impact. First, store relationships and resources. Keep walking with integrity, as integrity is the reputation you carry once the job stops.

The relationships you've built with mentors, sponsors, and colleagues might open doors to new opportunities. Be generous, store it well, and sow seeds whenever you can, because every seed you plant positions you for the future.

Let me introduce an additional framework I guide people through: the **Purpose Protection Plan**. Think of this as your guardrail:

1. **Align Skills:** Steward the gifts, talents, and experiences you already have so that what you do every day lines up with how God uniquely wired you.

2. **Anchor in Faith:** Ground your decisions, priorities, and responses in your relationship with God so purpose is led by conviction, not culture.

3. **Assign Purpose:** Intentionally connect your work, resources, and influence to a clear mission, instead of drifting through opportunities without direction.

4. **Diversify Streams:** Build multiple, aligned streams of impact and income so that one closed door never cancels your assignment.

5. **Detach Identity:** Refuse to tie your worth to titles, roles, or platforms, remembering that your true identity is in God and your purpose, not your position.

When I say "detach identity," I mean practice separating your self-worth from your job status, income, and title. This separation is essential to protect your peace and clarity.

Here are two stories that remind me that loss doesn't cancel destiny.

The first is about a corporate executive I consulted for over a year who was laid off during the mass tech firings. Her identity had been entirely built around her title, and the loss of her job left her feeling confused and depressed.

We worked together to change that. She launched a coaching program, spoke at local events, and wrote content based on her experiences. Within a year, she earned more than she had with her previous title and influenced people in ways she never could as a director.

The second story involves a single mother in one of my programs during the early COVID-19 lockdowns. Facing uncertainty about her next paycheck, she decided to use her cooking skills to deliver meals. She built a community group and now runs a small catering business along with kitchen training programs. She transformed necessity into legacy.

Now it's your turn. I encourage you to engage in a reflection and activation exercise called "Purpose if All Else Fails." Take some time right now to consider: if you lost your job tomorrow, what are three actions you would take in the first 30 days to continue walking on purpose or to begin doing so?

1. Identify the problem you'd solve.
2. Determine who you would serve.
3. Decide which platform you would activate.

Next, write your purpose statement in one sentence: "I was born to _____ so that _____."

Afterward, list the skills, relationships, and resources you already have that support this purpose. Which ones can you strengthen this week? Finally, identify one person who needs what you have to offer. Reach out to them and serve in that capacity.

To conclude this chapter, I want to affirm some declarations over you:

- I decree and declare that you are more than a conqueror.

- I decree and declare that you are not defined by past rejections.

- I decree and declare that your purpose is not determined by performance but is rooted in legacy and impact.

- I decree and declare that no corporate layoff can take away your calling or distract you from your purpose and destiny.

- I decree and declare that no retrenchment can alter who you were born to be.

- I decree and declare that although your job may change and your title may fade, your purpose and destiny remain, and your future is bright.

- I decree and declare that no weapon formed against you shall prosper.

- I decree and declare you are a purpose-driven warrior.

- I decree and declare that you will operate in excellence.

- I decree and declare that the world will hear your voice.

- I decree and declare the anointing of a builder upon your life, just like Nehemiah.

- I decree and declare faith over you, that you will walk in faith.

- I decree and declare that whatever is dormant within you that prevents you from walking on purpose will be activated.

- I decree and declare that excellence will be your portion.

Your job may change, and your title may fade, but your purpose is ingrained in your being. It cannot be erased. You can be fired from your job, but you can never lose your purpose.

Not every role, relationship, or assignment is meant to last forever. Some are seasonal; they exist for a specific purpose and time to prepare you, help you grow, or position you for the next chapter of your life.

For me, there were certain indicators that a role was seasonal and nearing its end. It often felt like the grace for it was lifted. What once flowed easily started to feel forced or heavy.

Another sign for me was realizing that I had learned the key lessons or gained the experiences that this role was meant to teach. Additionally, the role started to misalign with my core values, vision, and the direction that I felt God was leading me.

I also noticed that doors would begin to close naturally. Opportunities would dry up, relationships would shift, and my energy would fade. Instead of growth, I felt stagnation, which led me to believe my seasonal role was coming to an end.

Every season is about timing. Each season has an entry point and an exit point. Just as winter makes way for spring, God uses different seasons to prune, prepare, and transition us.

In discerning when a season is over, I look for patterns of change that keep surfacing, such as confirmations through prayer, wise counsel, or circumstances. You might sense a release in your spirit or a peace about moving forward, even into the unknown. Soon, new doors start to open that require your full attention. Staying in the same role then begins to cost you more than it grows you, and you'll definitely start to notice it.

Your ultimate purpose does not change; it is rooted in your identity. However, your assignments and the expressions of that purpose can change with the seasons.

For example, someone's purpose may always be to empower others. In one season, that might look like teaching; in another, it might take the form of building systems. In yet another season, it might involve mentoring the next generation. While the core purpose remains constant, how it is expressed can shift as you grow and as God expands your territory.

So, seasonal roles end when the lesson, impact, or assignment is complete, and seasons conclude when the timing shifts and God calls you forward. Your purpose is unchanging at its core, but how it manifests evolves across seasons, expanding as you do.

First, let's define some terms. A job is a position where you exchange your time, skills, or labor for income. While a job sustains you financially, it doesn't necessarily define who you are.

On the other hand, an assignment is a specific task or project assigned to you for a particular period. The focus of an assignment is to make a purposeful contribution in a specific context. Often, an assignment helps you grow and prepares you for what comes next in your journey.

Your calling, however, is the overarching purpose for which you were created. It represents your life's mission, grounded in your identity, values, and design. The focus of your calling is your destiny and the impact you make, which transcends different seasons of your life.

In summary, a job pays the bills, an assignment fulfills a temporary need, and a calling defines your ultimate "why" and life's work.

CHAPTER 13

LEAVING AN INHERITANCE: BUILDING WHAT OUTLIVES YOU

Let me make this plain and clear: this is not just a book.

This is a blueprint for a purposeful legacy. It's not merely about how to build a business or find your calling; it's about creating something that outlives you while walking in your purpose and destiny.

I didn't come this far just to come this far, and neither did you. I didn't write this book just to add another title to the market. I wrote it to change lives, empower hope, elevate destinies, and help people walk in their purpose.

This is not just for now but for what's next. You can lose your job, but you cannot lose your purpose. Let's discuss what legacy truly means.

Legacy is the imprint you leave on people and systems when you're no longer in the room. It's about what you instill in others that continues after you're gone. Now, hear me closely.

I am a mother, a leader, a sister, a friend, a mentor, and a daughter of the Most High God.

That is legacy. But I am also an innovator, a trailblazer, a disruptor, and a movement maker. I've built platforms, created businesses, and sold them. I lead organizations and sit on twenty-one boards, all designed to outlive my voice and presence. That is legacy.

So, I want you to ask yourself: are you building a brand or a bridge? Are you merely checking a box, or are you constructing change? One fades, while the other multiplies.

Next, let's talk a little about distractions. Sometimes, we don't realize we've been distracted until it's too late. I don't want you to lose sight of your destiny.

Distractions can pull us in many different directions. We're bombarded with announcements, alerts, notifications, and many other things vying for our attention. Some distractions come disguised as opportunities, but they can turn into detours.

We may say we're doing all the right things, but in reality, we're achieving nothing of real value. Let me teach you something I had to learn the hard way: there's a difference between what's right and what seems almost right.

Almost right is wrong. The "almost right" thing may keep you busy without fulfilling your purpose. It can trap you in relationship patterns that leave you emotionally distressed. Almost right is not right; it's a distraction from your destiny.

Don't confuse motion with mission. Almost right will have you going around in circles, ultimately leading you nowhere.

I want to remind you that I grew up in poverty in Houston, Texas. I had no generational wealth and limited access, but I did have the belief that my voice mattered, that my faith was not just private but strategic, and that my purpose was to build up, not blend in.

I've transitioned from operating in mediocrity to striving for excellence. This little girl from poverty now speaks on global stages, influencing politicians, governors, billionaires, policymakers, and CEOs while also empowering small business owners and underserved entrepreneurs. I aim to bridge the gap between the public and private sectors.

Faith is intertwined with my legacy. It serves as the blueprint of my legacy. Obedience unlocks overflow, and purpose compels us to walk in our destiny.

Now, if you're reading this and you lead a corporation, a government office, or a private foundation, or whatever it may be, hear me clearly.

We are no longer in the era of checkboxes. We're not interested in optics; we're here for outcomes.

Today's workforce, especially millennials and Gen Z, is seeking purpose-driven organizations. They want leaders who embody the change they believe in. The only way to retain them is to partner with leaders like myself, who are already building trust and making an impact in communities across the nation.

This is why organizations like JPMorgan Chase didn't just invite me to speak; they invested in me to help scale initiatives and move communities forward, along with many other organizations I could mention. This is also why I lead the Black Chamber of Arizona: they needed someone who could effectively bridge government, grassroots, and global business with credibility and purpose-driven leadership.

As a leader, I urge you to think about scale, impact, and generational legacy. Consider how the seeds you sow today will create a harvest for future generations.

True legacy is about inheritance. Proverbs 13:22 states, *"A good man leaves an inheritance to his children's children."* This isn't just about money; it's about wisdom, opportunities, mentorship, access to platforms, and systems. Let's frame it differently: You don't just build for the next generation; you must build with them in mind.

That's what legacy demands. So, I ask you: what will your children, community, and organization inherit because you obeyed your calling? Reflect on a few questions:

- What have you built that will endure after your name fades from the headlines?

- Are you creating moments or building movements?

- What systems are you leaving in place to empower the next leader?

- What knowledge or resources are you hoarding that you should be passing on?

Remember, legacy doesn't begin when you die; it starts when you choose to walk in purpose and destiny.

You are not average; you are an architect of change. You are not optional; you are ordained for such a time as this. You are not replaceable; you are essential in the marketplace.

Now is the time to build something that outlives you. You were never meant to blend in; you were born to walk in purpose and destiny. So rise.

If you're a public official, corporate executive, entrepreneur, or part of an organization ready to elevate your life or your organization, let's connect. You can invite me to speak, contract me to develop systems, license my curriculum, or bring me in to set up programs for your communities. Visit www.velmatrayham.com or scan the QR code. Together, we don't just build businesses; we build legacies and walk on purpose. You may be let go from your job, but you can never be fired from your purpose.

Some of the pitfalls that can hinder people from walking in their destiny include procrastination and delay. Many people put off important decisions, waiting for the perfect moment or seeking one more sign. This waiting often stalls their progress. It can also become a form of disobedience, leading to further delays.

Another significant pitfall is the fear of other people's opinions. The need for approval or the fear of rejection can prevent people from pursuing their purpose because they become trapped in the desire for validation. This limits their authenticity and binds them to the expectations of others.

Another common issue is falling into the comparison trap. When people focus on the journeys of others, it can lead to envy, insecurity, and even imitation. This comparison dilutes one's authenticity and delays personal purpose and destiny since everyone has a unique calling.

A lack of discipline and consistency is also a critical pitfall. Achieving one's purpose requires stewardship, and many fail to step into their full calling because they do not develop the necessary habits of focus and resilience. For example, it has taken consistent effort for me to stay committed to my responsibilities, such as completing this book and participating in calls, without making excuses.

Mismanaging seasons is another hurdle. Some people cling to expired assignments, which can confuse their understanding of their true calling. Staying in the wrong place for too long drains energy and hinders progress.

Additionally, surrounding oneself with the wrong relationships and environments can be detrimental. Being in the company of doubters, toxic influencers, energy drainers, or small-minded individuals can suffocate one's vision. Conversely, the right circle of people can accelerate personal growth and purpose.

Finally, disconnecting from God is a significant pitfall. Personally, I have noticed that when I don't pray for a few days, I start to feel spiritually disconnected. Purpose requires a divine alignment with the Creator, and maintaining that connection is crucial. Disconnecting spiritually leads to a loss of clarity, direction, and the power needed to fully walk in one's calling.

To conclude the chapter, I have a few key messages I want to convey to you. First and foremost, I want to leave you with a legacy of unwavering faith. It's important to trust God, even in uncertain times, and to remain anchored in your decisions, prayer, and faith.

My mother led with excellence, loved with compassion, and never wavered in her faith. Remember that true leadership involves stewardship, and faith is not just about beliefs; it's about how we live our lives.

Another important lesson is resilience. Life may knock you down, but you have to stand up even stronger. Understand that obstacles are not dead ends; rather, they are stepping stones to greater heights.

Lastly, it's essential to remember that life is made up of 10 percent of what happens to us and 90 percent of how we respond.

CONCLUSION

You made it. You didn't just read another book; you are now walking in divine purpose and destiny. Chapter by chapter, story by story, you answered the call to rise.

It's clear that you want to walk with purpose and destiny. You've wrestled with old mindsets, and if you've made it this far, I believe you have been set free.

The Bible tells us that whoever the Son sets free is free indeed. You may have faced failure, frustration, and the fear of starting over or not knowing how to walk in your purpose. You've dug deep into the words of this book and done the exercises. Now the real meaning of purpose-driven leadership is ready and alive within you.

So, let me remind you of something profound yet simple, something that can define your life:

You can be fired from your job, but you can never be fired from your purpose. This is not just a quote or the title of this book; it is divine revelation, a promise, and a mandate.

Thank you from the bottom of my heart. Before anything else, I want to express my gratitude. Thank you for allowing me to pour into you. Thank you for letting me walk alongside you. Thank you for giving yourself permission to believe again. Thank you for not quitting on your purpose, even when you had every reason to.

Thank you for daring to dream that your life could mean more than just existing. I don't take this time or your journey lightly. I don't take your pain for granted, and I absolutely don't take your purpose lightly.

What is within you is divine purpose. It may have been dormant, but I decree and declare that it is now awakened. Throughout this book, you've heard a lot about faith. You've learned about walking in purpose and destiny and have gone through exercise after exercise to develop practical next steps for navigating this journey we call life.

We've seen that failure is not failure; it is a stepping stone to keep moving forward. We've examined your environment and recognized the corporate resistance that disguises itself as silence and hijacking of destiny. We've discussed what it means to be a firebrand, not a leader who blends in, but one who burns brightly.

We've exposed evil gatekeepers, broken poverty mindsets, and distractions that delay destiny. We've walked through Nazareth seasons and experienced Arizona miracles. We've sown seeds, seen harvests, stepped into faith, and built systems that will outlive us.

This book serves as a blueprint for you and for the next generation. It is a reminder that you are not here just to fill space; you are created to solve problems.

So now, my beloved brothers and sisters, I invite you to rise, not next year, but today. You don't need to wait until the new year to create a new resolution. Your new beginning starts right now. It is time to step into the version of you that doesn't need a title to lead.

It's time to step into the space where your obedience creates abundance. It's time to embrace that God-assigned, world-changing, legacy-building purpose. Why? Because the world is not waiting for the next social media trend; it is waiting for you. The world needs you: your voice, your courage, your creativity, your systems, and, above all, your purpose-driven leadership. There are problems in this world that will remain unresolved if you don't take action.

Now, if you've ever thought, *Dr. Velma, I'm ready, but where do I start?* Let me provide a few paths for you to explore.

The Millionaire Mastermind Academy is a nonprofit organization dedicated to ending poverty through entrepreneurship. I created this nonprofit so that women from around the world and underserved communities could break free from the cycle of poverty and achieve sustainable entrepreneurial success, regardless of political circumstances.

To date, we've assisted over eight thousand entrepreneurs across the U.S. We've partnered with public and private corporations to create programs, mentorship opportunities, and access to capital, and you can be a part of this movement. Whether you're a corporate executive, a purpose-driven individual, or an emerging founder, there's room for you in this initiative. For more information, visit MillionaireMastermindAcademy.org.

You don't just need information; you need impartation that leads to transformation. That's why I host faith-based leadership intensives, VIP retreats, and executive-level coaching to help you align your assignments with your revenue model, multiplying both your impact and your income. If you're going to walk on purpose, you must be equipped mentally, spiritually, strategically, and physically.

Want to bring this experience to your city, company, or community? Let's discuss it! Visit www.velmatrayham.com for consulting, speaking, bulk book purchases, or licensing opportunities.

I work with small businesses, founders, corporations, city governments, and public agencies. I consult with C-suite executives and leadership teams on diversity, purpose-driven branding, equitable entrepreneurship, and career readiness. My curriculum is being used in municipal programs, universities, and corporate inclusion models across the country.

Whether you're ready to launch an economic empowerment initiative, license my purpose-driven training for your team, or book a keynote speaker who delivers impactful, measurable results, I am ready to serve. Visit www.velmatrayham.com for more details.

If you need prayer, I host a Friday morning battle-ready prayer call. You can find that information through the provided QR code at the beginning and end of this book.

Let me conclude with this: You were born on purpose, with purpose, for purpose. You are not an accident. There is nothing ordinary about you. You are the answer to someone's prayer and the solution to someone's problem. You are the leader someone has been waiting for. You are the legacy your bloodline needs, the generational curse breaker in your family.

Starting today, you no longer have to guess. No more confusion, no more delays, no more lack, and no more second-guessing your worth. Uncertainty ends here, and your assignment begins now. So, rise up, build what will outlive you, lead with purpose, and remember: you may be fired from your job, but you can never be fired from your purpose.

UNFIREABLE NOTES: A QUICK GUIDE

These are simple reminders to help you live what you just read. Come back to this page when you feel shaken, tired, or confused.

1. Purpose

- You can be fired from your job, but you can never be fired from your purpose.
- Your purpose is the problem God put you on earth to solve.
- Positions change. Titles change. Purpose does not.

Ask yourself:

- What problem keeps tugging at my heart?
- Who suffers if I stay silent?

2. Identity

- You are not your title, paycheck, or employer.
- Life is 10 percent what happens to you and 90 percent how you respond.
- You were born into a battle, but you are equipped to win.

Declare:

- My ending will not look like my beginning.
- I am more than a conqueror.
- I am the interruption to dysfunction in my family.

3. Generational Chains

- Generational curses are patterns—poverty, fear, addiction, small thinking—that try to repeat.
- They break when you see them, renounce them, and make different choices consistently.
- "It ran in my family until it ran into me."

Ask yourself:

- What cycles have tried to follow me into adulthood?
- What ends with me?

4. Failure and Finishing

- Temporary failure is not permanent defeat.
- Failure exposes what success often hides—your habits, your preparation, your identity.
- You are allowed to fail. You are not allowed to quit on your purpose.

Remember:

- Loss is not just pain; it is also data.
- You can start over smarter.

5. Entrepreneurship and Intrapreneurship

- Not everyone needs to own a company, but everyone is called to solve problems.
- Entrepreneurs build from the outside; intrapreneurs build from the inside.
- The greater the problem you solve, the greater the impact and income that can follow.

Ask yourself:

- Am I an entrepreneur, an intrapreneur, or both?
- How can I show up as a solution where I am right now?

6. Building and Scaling

- Businesses fail, pivot, grow, get sold—that does not change your assignment.
- Systems, strategy, and stewardship are how you scale purpose, not just passion.
- God trusted you with ideas, not just survival.

Remember:

- Start small. Start messy. Just start.
- Excellence is spiritual. Sloppiness is expensive.

7. Gatekeepers and Access

- Evil gatekeepers hoard access, spread lies, and protect broken systems.
- You have authority to expose, engage, empower, and establish new pathways.
- You are not begging for a seat; you are building new tables.

Ask yourself:

- Who have I allowed to define my limits?
- Where is God asking me to create something new instead of complaining?

8. Firebrand Leadership

- You were not created to blend in; you were created to burn bright.

- A firebrand carries the fire even when no one is clapping.
- True leadership is not about titles—it is about transformation.

Daily choices:

- Tell the truth, even when it costs you.
- Serve people, not just platforms.
- Refuse to shrink to make broken systems comfortable.

9. Prayer, Faith, and Work

- Prayer is not a backup plan; it is your battle plan.
- Faith without works is dead. Work without faith is empty.
- You do not harvest in the same season you plant.

Commit:

- To sow in prayer when no one sees.
- To obey even when you don't have the full picture.
- To keep moving, even when progress feels slow.

10. AI and the Future of Work

- AI can replace tasks and even positions. It cannot replace your purpose.
- You are not competing with AI; you are competing with the version of you that refuses to grow.
- Master the tools so you can stay focused on the assignment.

Ask yourself:

- What work am I still doing that a tool could help with?
- How can I learn enough to lead, not hide?

11. Being Truly Unfireable

To be unfireable does not mean people will never let you go. It means:

- If a door closes, you still have a calling.
- If a job ends, your assignment continues.
- If a title is stripped, your authority in God remains.

Daily declarations (adapt as your own):

- I can be fired from my job, but I cannot be fired from my purpose.
- I am a problem solver. I am a builder. I am a firebrand.
- I walk in purpose, on purpose, every day of my life.

Whoever the Son sets free is free indeed.
Walk like it. Decide like it. Lead like it.
You are unfireable.

WORK WITH DR. VELMA TRAYHAM

If this book spoke to you, imagine what can happen when we work together in real time.

I don't just write about purpose, economic mobility, and becoming unfireable—I build programs, companies, and movements that do it every day. From boardrooms to classrooms, from churches to city halls, my assignment is to help leaders turn disruption into destiny.

Keynotes and Live Events

Bring the Unfireable message to your audience through:

- Keynote talks and conferences

  Purpose-driven leadership, AI and the future of work, breaking generational poverty, entrepreneurship, and firebrand faith in business.

- Corporate and university events

  Leadership summits, ERG programs, commencements, orientation and career events, faith and marketplace gatherings.

- Church, nonprofit, and community events

  Economic empowerment, marketplace ministry, women's conferences, and purpose-intensive experiences.

Every message is customized to your audience, your goals, and your context.

Consulting and Advisory Partnerships

I work with public and private organizations that are serious about impact:

- AI and Unfireable Workforce Initiatives

  Helping companies and institutions prepare teams and communities for an AI-driven economy—without leaving people behind.

- Supplier diversity and small-business acceleration

  Designing and scaling programs that move underserved entrepreneurs from potential to contracts, from ideas to income.

- Purpose-driven strategy and culture

  Aligning vision, values, and systems so purpose is not a slogan—it shows up in hiring, budgeting, procurement, and community investment.

If you have resources but need a blueprint, that's where my team and I come in.

Programs and Ecosystem Building

Through ThinkZilla and Millionaire Mastermind Academy, we:

- Build award-winning accelerators that help entrepreneurs rise above poverty and access real opportunities.
- Partner with banks, corporations, universities, and government entities to design programs that create jobs, contracts, and legacy.
- Train leaders to build systems that outlive them and serve generations.

If you want to co-create something in your city, company, or campus, let's talk.

Booking and Contact

To book Dr. Velma Trayham for:

- Keynotes and speaking
- Executive or board strategy sessions
- Corporate, university, or government partnerships
- AI and economic empowerment initiatives

Please visit www.velmatrayham.com or https://unfireableofficial.com/

THANK YOU FOR READING MY BOOK!

Just to say thanks for buying and reading my book, I would like to give you a free Prayer Call, no strings attached!

Scan the QR code:

I appreciate your interest in my book and value your feedback, as it helps me improve future versions. I would appreciate it if you could leave your invaluable review on Amazon.com with your feedback. Thank you!